BEYOND ROADBLOCKS

Squibs and long shots 1984-2015

JONATHAN FALLA

Stupor Mundi
2017

Stupor Mundi was the name often given to the Holy Roman Emperor Frederick II of Hohenstaufen (d.1250). A man of great talents and learning, he was a lawgiver and patron of the arts and sciences, linguist and warrior whose Sixth Crusade retook Jerusalem by negotiation rather than bloodshed. His court at Palermo was described by Dante as 'the birthplace of Italian poetry.'

Also by Jonathan Falla

Fiction:

Blue Poppies
Poor Mercy
Glenfarron
The Physician of Sanlúcar
The White Porcupine
The Morena & other stories
Terraferma & other stories

Non-fiction:

The Craft of Fiction: how to become a novelist
True Love & Bartholomew: rebels on the Burmese Border
Ramón López Velarde: 21 Poems (translations)
Luck of the Devil: memoirs of Robert le Page (editor)
Hall in the Heart: A Fife parish hall and its community
Saama: Innocents in Asia

Drama:

Topokana Martyrs Day
The Hummingbird Tree
River of Dreams
Down the Tubes
Free Rope

THE AUTHOR

Jonathan Falla is an English writer, born in Jamaica but now living with his family in Scotland. His writing career has included several published novels, prize-winning drama for stage and film, and books on ethnography, international affairs, and music. As a paediatric nurse, he has worked for disaster and aid agencies in Indonesia, Uganda, Burma, Sudan and Nepal. He has held a scholarship at Cambridge, a Fulbright Senior Fellowship at the University of Southern California film school, and a writing fellowship of the Royal Literary Fund. In 2007 he was a Creative Scotland Award winner, and in the same year was shortlisted for the BBC National Short Story Prize. He lectures in Arts for the University of St Andrews and the Open University, and is Director of the Creative Writing summer school at St Andrews. He is also a musician performing with a professional early music group, and is a serving member of the Scottish Children's Panel.

Please visit: www.jonathanfalla.co.uk

Contents

INTRODUCTION

This collection brings together forty-eight occasional pieces written between 1984 and 2015, on subjects ranging from the music of forest rebels to Arabic novels, by way of Kenyan trains and the automatic pistols in my mother's attic.

My writing career began in 1981. I worked that year as a famine relief officer in Karamoja (eastern Uganda), and on my return home I turned my diaries into a play – *Topokana Martyrs Day* – a dark comedy about disaster field staff which received several productions in the UK and USA. Thereafter, I began to be invited to contribute articles to an eclectic variety of publications ranging from the *New Statesman* to *The Economist,* and from *Nursing Times* to the *Times Literary Supplement,* not forgetting niche outlets such as the *International Journal of Children's Rights* and *Eritrean Health News.*

The pieces gathered here are for enjoyment only; I've not included items that concern specific issues such as mental health services in Central America, nor specialist descriptions of music written to accompany recordings, nor many of the fifty reviews of books of fiction, history and world affairs. In one or two instances, however, a group of reviews fitted together, or a review and a lecture coincided, in which case I've conflated them.

I've done a little new editing on all these essays, to correct errors or to remove overlaps or particularly crass phrasing, and to make them more readable.

Backchat – 1984-5

I wrote these four items to commission for the 'Backchat' pages of the *New Statesman.* Aspects of these stories had already found their way into *Topokana Martyrs Day,* or would much later feature in my

2015 novel about revolution in Java, *The White Porcupine*. The essay on nursing education makes me cross to re-read even today. Some years after it was published, when I was re-training in paediatrics in Aberdeen, I was idly scratching behind my ear with a pencil and the lecturing doctor loudly asked me if I had nits. I was 35 years old and no, I didn't have nits, I was just bored.

The Revolution in Song – 1988

From 1982-86 I trained as a nurse, first in Oxford and then at the London Hospital for Tropical Diseases. As soon as I'd qualified, I went to Central America on a vague pretext of investigating possible projects for a new Nicaragua Health Fund. A consequence of the trip was an interest in the music of insurgencies – hence 'True Love & The Revolution in Song', published in the *Minnesota Review* in 1988 and quite bizarrely mis-edited. After obtaining recordings from various countries I had quite a collection of insurgent songs, which I donated to what is now the British Library Sound Archive in London. Of the two Nicaraguan singers encountered there, Salvador Bustos is I believe still alive and perhaps still playing, but Salvador Cardenal died in 2010 of a rare blood disease, aged just fifty.

Only the Sons of Shadow fear the Light – 1989

In February 1989, faced with the threat of the inundation of their lands by a proposed hydro-electric scheme, a large group of Amazonian indigenous peoples confronted government officials and power company engineers at a conference near Altamira (Brazil) sponsored by well-wishers such as Anita Roddick of The Body Shop. My sister-in-law Christine – an anthropologist turned GP – and I in my guise of tropical nurse were recruited to provide emergency health care, which happily was not needed. My account was published by the Catholic agency CAFOD soon after; it was something of a family affair, with my niece Harriet Logan taking the photographs. In the short term the protest was effective, with the hydroelectric scheme suspended. But the plans were redrawn and relaunched in spite of a second Indian gathering in 2008. Brazil's Supreme Court overturned objections, and construction began in 2011. Today, in 2017, work continues on what will be a colossal system of more than 400 dams, still vociferously opposed by environmentalists.

The Pocket True Love – 1996-7

In 1986-7 I worked as a health adviser with the Karen people in the forests on the Thai-Burma border (I can't get used to calling it Myanmar). The Karen had been at war with the Burmese government for some four decades and their culture had steadily adapted to the purposes of ethnic rebellion. Later, working in a chilly loft over a shed in the Scottish Highlands, I wrote an account of the Karen which was published by Cambridge University Press as *True Love & Bartholomew: Rebels on the Burmese Border.* In 1996-7 I gave talks derived from this on a local radio station, Heartland FM in Pitlochry, and 'The Pocket True Love' is the text of these.

What do they think they're doing? – 1997

Although I worked for various aid agencies between 1978 and 1991, several essays reflected my growing disenchantment with aid and development projects, and my thoughts about the role of aid workers in society. These include 'What do they think they're doing?' from the *Times Literary Supplement.*

The Desert & the River Dee – 2002

This essay looks at two Sudanese novelists with considerable reputations in English, Tayeb Salih and Leila Aboulela. I wrote this while working on my own novel set in Sudan (*Poor Mercy,* 2005) and the essay was published in Susan Hill's magazine *Books and Company* in 2002. Leila kindly contributed her endorsement to the cover of *Poor Mercy* and we later shared a platform at a book event in Edinburgh, just at the time of the uprising against President Mubarak of Egypt. Something of the squabbling exiles described in her novel *Minaret* reappears in my sixth novel *Good News from Riga.*

Scotland on Sunday – 2002-06

For a few months I had a weekly column in the magazine section of *Scotland on Sunday* – the weekend companion to *The Scotsman* – but already the newspapers were feeling the challenge of the internet. Costs rose, circulation fell, and the magazine was axed entirely before the last of these short pieces made it into print. A number of the essays refer directly or indirectly to my books and the journeys behind them, such as the trip to Patagonia which inspired my fourth novel *The Physician of Sanlúcar.*

What you seek is what you'll get – 2002-06

Scotland on Sunday also commissioned most of my later book reviews, until book sections became a disposable luxury for the Scottish press. 'Among Muslims' and 'All News out of Africa is Bad' consider two preoccupations in the books received.

Meddling in Darfur – 2005

In July 2005, the 31st G8 summit was convened at Gleneagles (Scotland) by Tony Blair, with a special mission to discuss poverty and national debt in Africa. Only one actual African (Thabo Mbeki) was invited. Edinburgh City Council responded to the G8 with lectures and debates, exhibitions and workshops, while 200,000 people marched through the town under the slogan 'Make Poverty

History'. A series of evening talks called 'The Edinburgh Africa Conversations' was held at the Tron Theatre, of which I gave one, 'Out of control in Darfur'. At much the same time I had written a review for *Scotland on Sunday* of a memoir by Claire Bertschinger of her career in disaster relief, as well as contributing an essay to the online literary magazine *Textualities* (May 2005) which describes the African genesis of my novel *Poor Mercy* published that summer. There was some overlap between these so, rather than re-print all three, I've conflated the review, the essay and the article into one, 'Meddling in Darfur.'

Michael Riviere: Mutability in Norfolk – 2005

Michael Riviere was the father of an old friend of mine from Cambridge. I stayed in the family's supremely peaceful Norfolk house on many occasions. In his retiring, dignified way, Mick was a fine poet and translator. This survey of his work comes from *Poetry Salzburg Review*.

Corvaceous – 2008

In 2008, after a tedious search for a publisher, my third novel *Glenfarron* was published by Two Ravens Press in Ullapool, Scotland. At the same time, I wrote articles for an online literary magazine from Two Ravens called *Corvaceous* which didn't survive long, brought down like so many small publications by laggard contributors who would not get their pieces in by deadline.

Historical fiction and the moral agenda – 2014

In 2014 a festival of Historical Fiction was held at Summerhall in Edinburgh. Although I've never thought of myself as an historical novelist, nonetheless several of my novels have particular period settings. This was a lecture given at the festival and later repeated for St Andrews

Spectrum – 2015

This last essay – on fine printing of literature – was commissioned for the web pages of the Royal Literary Fund, for whom I had worked as an academic writing skills consultant posted to Dundee University for three years. It was published online in 2015.

BACKCHAT

1. GATE CRASHING THE KRATON

My friend Zamzami comes from Cirebon, on the north coast, and at Cirebon there is a palace or *kraton*. Java still has a few such *kratons*, the Republic of Indonesia tolerating the redundant sultans, the local people doting on them. Zamzami decided he would take me to Cirebon for *Sekaten,* the celebration of the Prophet Mohammed's birthday.

In other towns, *Sekaten* is now a tourist attraction. At Cirebon it's for the locals in their thousands.

A fair gathers before the *kraton* gates. You have to like people and share the Javanese taste for close proximity; they tend to compress themselves into the smallest space available. At nightfall, as the swarm gathered, mere movement through the tight mass became a sport in itself. Youths formed chains, hands on shoulders, and just for the hell of it jogged into the dark pack, out the other side, back in again. A 'mini-train' did the same thing, ruthlessly, laden with screaming girls and two young men standing on the tractor waving torches and blowing whistles. Stalls lit by scores of fierce white pressure lamps cooked and flogged everything imaginable, exacerbating the night heat. Two dwarfs danced on top of a lorry to advertise a tonic wine.

But *Sekaten* is a deeply serious affair. Javanese rulers radiate a spiritual force and the closer you are the more you will physically absorb. Zamzami pulled me through the *kraton* courtyards – dank and unlit, and cut about by fragmentary crumbling walls – to the single-storey hall of heirlooms: canon, musical instruments, pikes and daggers, a carriage shaped like the mythical bird Garuda, and dark wooden chests. Each of these artefacts, being the property of the Sultan, is therefore a repository of power, and the hot storerooms were thick with incense and the poor who had paid to come, each person carrying a rag which they rubbed over the heirlooms, then over their own faces. The queue wound through the palace into the audience hall where elderly palace servants wrapped in old batik, sweating by pressure lamps, sat in silence as the populace came through rubbing everything in sight, even the door knobs.

Zamzami and his well-educated brother were embarrassed.

'What are they doing?' said Zamzami, almost as though he'd never been there before. His brother had an answer:

'These are not Cirebon. These are ignorant people from the villages.'

We fought our way out past a bamboo cage in which villagers could pay to sit all night, close to the source of power.

The following day, prior to the Sultan's procession, we drove out of town to a sacred spring where sages accepted gratuities and heard requests by a small, profoundly unimpressive pool with a standpipe gurgling into it. There was a tomb close by.

'A prophet,' said Zamzami.

'No, a hero, Prince Siliwangi,' said his brother.

No matter who: this was another source of power. Boys sold small plastic jerrycans to be filled with holy water. Vast women launched into the pool, stripped to the waist. The boys gawped at the enormous breasts and whispered, 'Wow, look at that milk!'

Zamzami grumbled at the faithful gulping the water:

'Oh, my God, they believe it.'

But when, in the evening, we tried to return to the *kraton* to see the procession to the Sultan's mosque and the blessing of the heirlooms, we were deeply disappointed to find that we could come nowhere near the gates. The crowd was impacted; the stone walls had sprouted a human foliage. Police and soldiers stood across the road, eyeing the people warily.

'Ridiculous,' said Zamzami. 'It gets worse every year.'

'We'll get in,' said his brother, 'if we use him.' He was pointing at me.

The two of them strode up to the nearest soldier.

'This (*they lied*) is an official from the British Embassy in Jakarta. You must help.'

And help the soldiers did, waving us through the cordon and standing us conspicuously under the archway. At which moment the crowd's hysteria mounted – not, I was relieved to see, in rage, but in excitement: the procession was coming. The soldiers fought to keep the road to the mosque open, waving their rifles, smacking heads and yelling, 'Sit down!' until the crowd at last all did. I cowered behind the gate hinges. But then the Sultan himself appeared, and instantly everyone produced their rag and waved it frantically overhead to soak up his radiant power.

'Ridiculous,' muttered Zamzami again in my ear.

'Come inside the gate, sir,' called a soldier.

15

The procession, headed by an engaging mix of girl guides and elderly palace officers in batik, bore the entire stock of palace heirlooms to the mosque for blessing. Fine featured and expressionless, the Sultan and his family walked behind followed by retainers bringing palanquins of food. There was an extraordinary shabbiness; everything, even the retainers' jackets, looked worn out.

They all disappeared into the mosque and at once the problem that gripped the whole assembly was: How to get out. Our pole position disadvantaged us now, but the soldiers began yelling again: a motorcade was coming, crawling out of the *kraton* gates honking furiously. With delightful irreverence the crowd climbed on board the cars. Zamzami helped me up, and thus it was that a fake British embassy official rode out of Cirebon *kraton* sitting on the bumper of a Javanese general's Mercedes.

2. BEYOND THE ROADBLOCKS

I'd never been to Africa before. The idea faintly bored me; lots of zebras and wildebeest, no doubt, but my interest in game was slight. There's be none of that high-octane culture I'd thrived on in Asia. Furthermore, the Uganda Airlines Nairobi-Entebbe flight was two hours late.

'They're probably looking for some petrol,' griped an English banker.

'Or the aeroplane,' sighed his pal.

'No, that's just round the corner, came last night. Usual story: the pilot gets so pissed they don't see him before ten. For a so-called international bloody airline…'

It was also called Magendo Airlines, *magendo* meaning black market. The banker offered me a place on a charter flight, $70 return.

'It goes when we say go,' he stabbed, 'and go is what we ought to do, all of us, UN, aid agencies, finance, the lot. Leave them to rot in their own hell for six months.'

A fair hell it sounded. Amin was gone but Milton Obote was fast proving himself Big Idi's equal. The official opposition was daily crushed further underfoot. The unofficial opposition blew up Kampala's generators by night. A large tract of the country was starving, which was why I'd come. This I'd learned in England.

Things improved in the air, in a pleasant little Fokker high over Lake Victoria. Times were hard; the in-flight snack was a dry roll and a banana. But I cheered up and drifted peaceably off to sleep.

17

Collected from Entebbe in the agency pickup, I was introduced to roadblocks. The first was police, and they only wanted a lift into Kampala for 'a fellow officer.' The second was the Tanzanian army [of occupation]. Alice, my Baganda escort, refused to speak Swahili, so we were searched. The third was Ugandan troops, and perfunctory.

'Roadblocks are a way of paying the soldiers,' Alice said. 'At night the soldiers are scared and hide in the bushes. The 'block' is a stick across the tarmac. If you don't see it and don't stop, they shoot.'

We drove to a villa, base camp for itinerant expatriates involved in Uganda's mess. Aid teams, United Nations, a reporter from Swedish television who'd lost his cameraman. Beautiful gardens, a parrot, an armed policeman at the gate.

'He'd be the first to run,' they said.

At other embassies, extra grilles and fences were being installed; the British put up engagement photos of Charles and Diana. There were rumours of an American evacuation plan.

I registered, then went for my first stroll in Africa. Most shops were closed, many were burnt out; just a few struggled on. Police and troops were everywhere, all with automatic weapons, each with four or five clips of ammunition held together with rubber bands. Near the bus terminal a Police Land Rover had been stopped by soldiers in red berets. A crowd spectated from a 'safe' distance, the passers-by turning to watch, quiet but poised, moving slowly closer. Then, a single shot; flight reflexes in unison, the formerly upright crowd went past me at a slope, running. The moment passed; I didn't look back.

Throughout the afternoon someone in Stockholm kept calling the Swede, but he was at Entebbe airport looking for his cameraman. At 6:30 the cameraman phoned, alarmed; they'd missed each other, it was getting dark, and no one in their right mind went out after dark in Kampala. Gilbert, my agency's field officer, declared that we'd go and get him, touting for company by calling the exploit 'short and dodgy.'

We left at 7:45, driving past the old Kotolo airstrip and several roadblocks, with nervous soldiers in the dark. Gilbert invariably called out, 'Good evening, how are you?' and we were invariably waved through. We found the cameraman and loaded him in, all of us quietly dropping things, jumpy. Back past a few drunks, and the first roadblock.

'Good evening, how are you? We are going home.'

'What are you carrying?'

'A friend and his suitcase. Nothing more.'

The enormous TV camera crouched in the dark between our legs. We drove alongside the airstrip, slowing towards the next roadblock – and then we were being shot at, bullets coming out of the dark across the grass. Gilbert hesitated, uncertain whether to risk provoking fire from the roadblock as well by accelerating away. But the soldiers, scared witless, yelled:

'Go on, go on!'

Which we did.

'Heads down, chaps,' called Gilbert, who had been a Tanks officer.

The cameraman's boss arrived home just behind us in another Land Rover now with drilled windows. The cameraman had, by great foresight, brought us a bottle of whisky. I began to wonder whether seats were still available on the banker's return charter. All night there was sporadic gunfire, rain, squealing cars, and lightning.

I did fly next day. Gilbert took me right across Uganda in his own little four-seat Cessna. At 7,000 feet, features have features, not merely form. I could lean out and shake the farmers' hands. Uganda was displayed to me, battered but still fertile, its superstructure gone berserk but its heart still beating, even if survival meant selling the coffee *magendo*. We came to a game park, flying low, startling out from under the trees all those animals I thought lived in Hollywood – lions, buck, zebra and elephants. I'd imagined them to have all been slaughtered but here they were, and the famine-struck region looked as green as green. I'd never seen anything quite so lovely.

Clearly, Africa was going to take some getting used to.

3. PLAYING WITH WAZUNGU

KENYA (Nairobi-Mombasa train): At nightfall, Fisher, whom I had never met before, sat down with me at the only remaining table in the dining car and asked what I was reading – which was the Oxford 'Standard' Swahili dictionary, a title whose arrogance is only partially mitigated by its being the only decent dictionary available.

'Ah, yes, now then,' he said, and took the dictionary from me as he settled. He matched the ancient rolling stock better than I, his caricature ex-RAF manner, tropical suit and cravat with Spitfires quite in place with the rich purple plush and mahogany fittings, tended by black servants. Personally I prefer the other dining car on the line, the one with glass partitions engraved with East African birds.

'Listen to this.' He turned the pages. 'I'll bet you've never realised how many other uses the Swahili have for the word *mzungu*.'

'It means a European,' I offered, half-listening, watching the buck, giraffe and zebra swerving away from the line and bolting for the horizon in the dusk over the grey-fawn upland plain.

'But listen!' he insisted. '*Mzungu* – also, the picture cards in a playing deck. English kings and queens, for God's sake!'

And knaves, of course. Two-dimensional foreign oppressors in flash regalia. Fisher read on.

'Or it means, "something wonderful, startling, surprising, ingenuity, cleverness" – synonymous with European, you see?'

He sipped his Tusker beer. The next meaning that he read out, however, threw a different shadow.

'*Mzungu* – any device or expedient for getting out of a difficulty.'

Skulking deviousness, the capture of the citadel by a ruse, betrayal of allies, welching on a treaty. This, it seemed, came naturally to Europeans, as Fisher pronounced:

'*Mzungu* – instinct in animals, as in, "every bug follows its *mzungu*."'

He paused, wondering if that could possibly be a slur on the hygiene of himself and other settlers who had stayed on – but then thankfully remembered the young tourists, the Great Unwashed sunning themselves on the coast at Malindi.

'Is that the lot?' I asked.

'By no means. Listen: "In the plural, *wazungu* – the teachings given to young girls when they reach puberty or in initiation rights." As in, I suppose, "Don't play with your *wazungu* or you'll go blind, or worse!" Ha ha!'

The waiter, a deferent teenager in immaculate but overlarge whites, took our order. Fisher, studiously not looking at him, called for fried fish.

'Served, inevitably, with cassava. Which,' he triumphed, 'is the final meaning of *mzungu* – a type of cassava.'

A root vegetable which must be carefully boiled to remove the Prussic acid. Was that how Kenyans saw us, then? Something to be pulled up out of the dirt, chockful of poison but sadly necessary to the economy? Fisher drank down his Tusker and spoke for a while of things he appreciated: giraffes, Cambridge architecture, choral polyphony in Kings chapel. I looked at the passing landscape and remarked on how much I was enjoying the journey. This was a mistake; he was less than content.

'Bloody lights don't work in my compartment. Which is just Kenya, isn't it? I suppose the bulbs blew sometime last year.'

Still, I said, he could hardly fail to enjoy the scenery.

'Even that can get oppressive. We have a phrase for it: MMBA.'

I looked suitably blank.

'Miles and miles of bloody Africa.'

At this point the fish arrived and Fisher immediately lost his temper.

'Christ, this muck is boiled!'

The outburst was sufficient to drive the young waiter back in confusion. The Chief Steward came to his rescue.

'My sincere apologies, sir; there has been an error. May I offer you fried chicken?'

Fisher grumpily assented. It was now almost dark outside, and the wind was flapping the purple curtain in his face. He tried unsuccessfully to tuck it back, then snapped a finger at the waiter.

'Close this.'

The boy leaned across the table and grasped the top of the wooden louvred shutter. But it was stuck, and his slight figure and awkward position made it impossible for him to raise it. He stood back uncertainly. Fisher at last looked straight at the black.

'I said, close it.'

The boy tried again but with no success. Fisher bawled, 'Christ, does nothing work on this bloody train?' and, slamming his hand hard up against the slats, freed the shutter and sent it upwards. The boy could not remove his fingers in time: they were caught and crushed at the top. Whipping his hands back, he hugged them to his belly and staggered weeping into the kitchen.

'Right.'

Fisher sat back and his manner altered instantly as he turned again to consider the works of God and man.

'Ah, you know, I have often thought of the giraffe's neck in terms of Gothic flying buttresses...'

4. CUT-OUT ANGELS

I've completed three years at an internationally reputed centre of nursing education. I cannot recommend the education, although anyone might enjoy helping the sick to feel better. My problems began before the course started; my place was vetoed by the occupational health doctor on unspecified medical grounds which she couldn't divulge. These turned out to be my sex, my age [28, in 1982], and my university degree. Another graduate was told she was 'potentially anorexic'. She fought her way in too.

First came the introductory school, six weeks in the classroom learning basic skills. We injected oranges and brushed each other's teeth. Our doubts grew; there can be few more ludicrous sights than a score of young adults sitting in silent rows watching a tutor solemnly soaping down a plastic dummy on a bed. Then the staff doctor returned to give us the tail-end of Matron's morality:

'Some of you will get boyfriends, I'm sure, but I just want to tell you that you don't have to say "yes".'

The lectures began – day after day, hour after hour. Who invented the overhead projector? They should be shot. The whirring fan, the glaring screen numbed the enquiring mind, propelling us through a dilute medical syllabus as in a trance. Somebody once remarked that the lecture method is the most efficient yet devised for transferring notes from the teacher's book to the students' files without passing through the brains of either. Like zombies we sat, thankful for simple instructions such as 'You may put your pencils down now'. When the doctors came to talk about specialities we woke up a bit, but when one of them noticed a textbook on my desk and said,

'Well, you're a bright boy with a big book', I was by then too enfeebled to walk out.

There were films. In the 'paediatric module' we had one about infant nutrition – parents extolling the quality control at the Heinz factory. What followed: healthy debate? A few guarded qualifications from our tutors? No, just a pamphlet hymning a certain brand of baby's toothbrush. The students' exasperation peaked. One sat knitting a jumper in the shape of a bat, another took out her Nikon and took portrait photos of her class neighbours. We made a visiting tutor cry. I'm certainly not proud of that but, as the Senior Tutor raged at us for behaving like juveniles, I wondered how it was I'd got through four years of university without similarly regressing.

It used to be said that nurses are not required to think, only to carry out instructions, but to experience brain-jamming in lieu of education is maddening. One colleague queried divergences between textbook and tutor (wondering which to follow with real patients), was taken aside and warned against arrogance. I myself faced an enquiry for undermining Sister's authority in front of the patients on a psycho-geriatric ward; I'd pointed out that all the staff were misnaming a drug. Another misguidedly remarked to a tutor that she'd actually managed to do more work (extra bed baths) than instructed by the nurse in charge, and was threatened with disciplinary action.

A telegram came from Canada; a student's father was dying. She flew home in a hurry, leaving a letter for the school. On her return she was 'counselled' i.e. berated for not having asked permission to go. This was not professional, they cried. On qualifying, the nurse took her professional skills straight back to Canada, both bereaved and appalled by the flagrant contradiction of anything they'd ever taught about compassionate understanding.

26

Back in 1978, a Royal College of Nursing reported castigated hierarchical didacticism, failures of confidence and heavy-handed discipline in counselling of students. Florence Nightingale called nursing a fine art. What we saw was the demoralisation of intelligent adults who had voluntarily gone into vocational training, the bludgeoning of alert minds freely offered for the relief of human suffering. Most nurses desire the self-respect bestowed by a professional skill and yet constantly fail to stand up for themselves in the face of condescension – which is hardly surprising, as they start their careers cowed by their own tutors. It is thought [in 1985] that 45% of nurses smoke, and a researcher told us that it was the strain of observing so much death. None of us believed her.

I have sympathy for any teacher who has to 'get through the material', a prescribed syllabus to a pre-ordained schedule. For every 'module' there was an official list of objectives, and the tutors had little choice but to plough on – but when so little is being absorbed that the lecture has to be repeated a year later, the system is manifestly failing. We tried to add a little leaven to the mix. We suggested visits to laboratories, to a *post mortem*. We requested a visit from Training in Race & Health. We did a get a delightful acupuncturist. Some of us ran evening discussions in conjunction with a group of medical students, with classy guest speakers on industrial radiation, holism, and racism in the NHS. Few tutors came – but I'd not do their job either: underfunded, understaffed, the internationally reputed school is chronically short of paper. Nurse tutors have been through the mind-mangle themselves; it would be a dauntless soul who tried to change (not merely 'upgrade') that massy institution, though a few do try. In the teeth of this primitive pedagogy they talk now of making the course 'more academic'.

So, now we're finished, we're qualified professionals. But ten out of the twenty-seven in the class have dropped out, and half of the remainder have declined any of the jobs the training hospital offers. We just don't want to work there any more.

THE REVOLUTION IN SONG

1986 was my year for seeing revolutions, and all three of them were in fine voice. In El Salvador the civil war had reached a stalemate but, even in government-held territory, they sang hymns that might be thought thoroughly subversive. In Nicaragua the initial fight was won and the more bombastic lyrics stilled also; now they crooned more pensively over the more intractable problems that obstructed their millennium. In Burma they had been at each other's throats for decades, but in a low key, and so the songs were an insistence: yes, there *is* a revolution and it may drag on rather but it'll not go away and you'll not forget us, will you? Not if we keep singing.

I had an invitation from a priest, a Spaniard who believed that his nationality gave him at least partial protection from the death squads of El Salvador. There was to be a weekend of music in the hills, a 'workshop', and it could be remarkable. If it worked out well we'd see, for a change, the poor risking a little communal joy. That would be a change, certainly. We'd visited Salvador's slums, refuges and refugee settlement schemes and there not much joy to be found there. I got the idea: music as a liberating force, at the heart of popular solidarity.

We drove out of the city up steep dirt tracks, the bus near toppling, lopsided under its roof load of youth and guitars. Very bad roads; very hot, very dry, very bumped about, we came along high ridges running away from the capital amongst the interminable coffee groves that do not belong to the cultivators, the bushes all dark green and dusty. At the top end of the ridge was a small town with a rather grand new cement church – a foreign mission.

Rather more than one hundred participants turned up, kids in large part from different towns but none the less welcome for the spark they brought. More than half brought guitars also. The programme was simple enough. For three or four hours a day over the long weekend we sat on the cement seating behind the altar while a priest with an accordion taught us hymns. We began on the Friday evening with 'Glory to you for evermore':

Gloria a ti por siempre, por siempre – ¡por SIEM-PRE!

Two hard guitar chords hit the last syllables over and again. It was fun, at least for an hour or so.

We were divided into eight groups: Lambs, Little Angels... I forget the others. We had allotted tasks. I was cast among the *Angelitos* and we had to enforce discipline. I am not even a Christian, though I was school headboy once. The Lambs I think got to clean the latrines; others cooked, or swept. The priests had devised games and activities for us. We enacted, *en masse,* the stages of the Mass, and were told its meaning. We fell upon a heap of newspapers and cut them up into order to illustrate Sin, which was most interesting, for the young Salvadorean is perfectly aware that one should not believe everything one reads in the papers. We stuck our cut-out vice onto large sheets of sugar-paper for each other's contemplation and, amongst the rapes, the murders and the frauds of Mammon, there were the lies, distortions, and all the misrepresentations of a smug and reactionary press.

'You see here? It says that people are falling into debt through drink and idleness but that's a lie, that's not why our families get into debt and the newspapers know it so for them to say so, that's a lie!'

Right enough. We picked up our guitars again, banging out that double strum:

Gloria a ti por siempre, por siempre – ¡por SIEM-PRE!

What was going on, exactly? Could this be regarded, really, as the foundation of group consciousness among the oppressed? I was taken in hand not by one of the priests but by a sympathiser.

'You have to understand so much first.'

Well, but we only have a few days. What is it that I'm looking at?

'But yes, you must understand. You must know what the situation is here. This part of the country was the worst hit in the *Matanza* [a military massacre that crushed a peasant uprising in 1932, killing possibly 40,000]. These people have had the shit beaten out of them for centuries, they are more demoralised than you can begin to know. Just to get them here, singing together, is an act of popular unity.'

But we're just learning hymns and dogma.

'The Fathers would like to do much, much more. But look at the numbers who have come! They didn't expect anything like so many, and who knows who they are? Certainly there are *Ojos* here.'

The *Eyes,* spies of the Army and the hit squads and the secret terror.

'You see? They have to be very careful what they say. Just to work for unity and self-respect among the poor like this is a subversive act now. You see that old wooden house over there? The shop? That was the home of a great popular leader. Of course it is not marked. What can we do to keep that spirit alive?'

Gloria a ti ¡por SIEM-PRE! That, and other hymns also now, booming out of the big cement hall. There was a call for different hymns, and a sheet of words was handed out in the middle of which, hedged about, half-buried in peasant canticles, were one or two that hit a vigorous note of protest: of dispossession, the blood of our fathers, the broken backs of our mothers. As it happened we didn't get to learn that one. The Eyes and the Ears, *Ojos* and *Orejas* everywhere.

From time to time I walked up and down the main street of the little hill town to look about: the coffee groves and the clouds below the ridge; the long narrow valleys leading out of the capital, San Salvador; the slick highway to the airport – all glimpsed between the houses strung along the bluff. Their tall and grandiose weatherboard façades and tiled front rooms had definite pretensions to gentility, but their undercrofts behind, on the falling slope of the hill, were heaped with broken cartwheels and pig litter, dark and alive with cockroaches. On other hillsides, not so far off, the Air Force was attempting to bury the FMLN guerrillas by lifting the fields into the air with high explosive and dropping them back onto the villagers. You could often hear or even see the bombing from the capital.

I stopped and talked to the village pharmacist. No, there was no one really to care for the people here. There was a doctor who came occasionally and held clinics; the last had been part of a flying visit by the Army, literally flying in helicopters, in pursuit of 'hearts and minds'. To the little girls they'd given dolls; to the little boys they'd given toy guns; to everyone they'd given pills – and then they'd flown away again.

Back in the mission compound, as the day began to fail they'd emerged for a break. The priest with the accordion had a headache, the fifty or sixty guitarists had sore fingers, the singers sore throats;

we needed our evening meal. The kitchen squad came in with pans of that unavoidable Central American combination, rice, beans and tortillas. Stiff and saturated with hymns, we wanted relaxation. The guitars were hung up under the verandah, a few of the musicians flaked out on the rows of mattresses inside. We all sat about eyeing each other, chewing tortillas, wondering how to unwind.

There were a few older people there, and one or two were fine musicians of the campo, their fiddles and a squeezebox a welcome leaven to the massed guitars. A clump of three or four men stood together and began to play 'village music' – a foxtrot, in fact, but it had been played in and around his village all his life.

Nothing more indigenous?

'I tell you, these people have had the shit knocked out of them! You look: they are just beginning to relax here. It's so painfully slow. They've learned to trust this mission just a little now.'

Why does it have to be foreign priests, imported along with the accordion?

'There are some fine, selfless Salvadorean priests, but not so many. Some will not come out to these villages at all because the people can pay them nothing. These Europeans, though, will not take a collection in church from people who have so little already.'

The company was beginning to relax at last. The old men standing together were now tapping their feet, staring at the ground with an appreciative musical smile as they absorbed and approved their fiddling friend's lilt. They began to add on – a squeezebox, another fiddle, a round country ukulele in the dusk.

Then there came a new voice singing: 'Let's pull the ox from the ravine!' A hit song:

33

¡Sacaremos ese buey de la barranca!

The Spanish phrase implies, 'Let's do our best to pull this thing off.' Not at first sight a great lyric, but it had caught on. It was the young who were relaxing now, and this was their latest, a tune rather like our 'Heads and shoulders, knees and toes'. It escalated. The guitars came off the verandah wall again and as the lights came on the catchy tune spread among the people.

¡De la barranca sacaremos ese buey!

There was no shortage of verses to the song, apparently. Like a taut E-string unwinding, the children suddenly eased out of their earnestness. Five, ten guitars took it up together, while the guitar-less beat their hands on any surface that presented: Let's pull that ox from that ravine! The old fiddlers dropped their foxtrot and threw in their lot with the hit. The fast, snappy beat took a hold and we began to dance, more and more of us packing in under the lights of the verandah, forming into circles, bouncing and clapping, jumping on toes, stamping and shouting and beaming sweaty, hugely excited grins. Round and round the chorus: Pull out the ox! Except that it transpires that the wretched brute was never in the ravine at all, but was lurking in the brush nearby – and so, in vengeful pique, let's push the bloody animal down there:

¡Meteremos ese buey a la barranca!

Come Sunday morning, solemnity was restored. Mass was sung. And then a session of self-criticism. The eight groups – Little Angels, Lambs of God, Candelabras and all – packed onto the cement benches and told each other hard truths. The catering had been fine but the Lambs had made a pig's dinner of the latrines. It was wonderful to have new insights into Sin, and into the Mass. But discipline?! *Madre.* We Little Angels, we had to confess, had not

34

pulled our weight. In the dormitories, exhausted guitarists had been kept awake half the night by giggling. It was not on.

As a finale we banged out that hymn again. That at least had been learnt. The stages of the Mass had been learnt (even I knew them now). What of liberating solidarity had been achieved? In truth, only what I'd been told. Was I too much of an outsider after all? It had, been enjoyable, certainly, but were things what they seemed? Or rather: were they perhaps exactly what they seemed? Was this not just straight evangelism?

Back in the capital, I bought a cassette recording of the *Barranca* song. It had to be admitted that, of the Ox and the Lamb, the Ox had the edge in rhythm. But from time to time I do still hit those two guitar chords:

Gloria a ti ¡por SIEM-PRE!

'The Guitar in Arms' was an instrument of the Nicaraguan revolution from the outset. Illiterate insurgents encouraged and instructed each other in song. And I bought the LP records of that also. *La Guitarra Armada* includes music by many of the outstanding names of Nicaraguan '*nueva cançion*' (new song). The lyrics might tell you, for instance, how to strip a machine gun, and they would insist that, however miserable it might be holed up on a hillside watching the dictator Somaza's bravos decapitate your father and rape your mother, victory would surely come. Which, of course, in July 1979 it did. It's all on record, and many of them are very rousing songs – even if, as a popular refrain, the reiterated phrase 'Sandinista 19th of July Youth!' lacks charm or interest to my ear.

By the time I got to Nicaragua seven years later, the music was perceptibly changing. You could still hear the old songs, you could still buy the records, but tub-thumping battle hymns were now sung more by Salvadoreans in exile – their battle far from over – than by Nicaraguans who preferred to put the troubles of inflation, the *contras,* and shortages of beef and beer behind them of a Saturday night and hurl themselves around the dance floor to dreadfully secular salsa and *costeño* music from the Caribbean side of the beleaguered country. The hottest hit was a song in English which simply extolled bananas:

> All the people like banana,
> Everybody like banana.
> White man like it, colour man like it, China man like it…

Like the ox in the ravine, it had an edge of danceability over the heavy stuff.

Nueva cançion is not a Nicaraguan invention; the Left in Latin America has been writing good songs for a long time. In Allende's Chile, song flourished as never before. Argentina's Mercedes Sosa must count as one of the most compassionate singers alive – which, if some of her outraged compatriots had their way, she wouldn't be. [She died in 2009] Surely, I thought, the New Nicaragua could manage something a little subtler than a harmonised armourer's manual and a paean to bananas?

In Managua I was invited to a little act of commemoration for Camillo Torres, a Colombian priest who some twenty years before had finally reconciled his faith with bloodshed in defence of the poor, only to be killed a week or two after taking up arms [in 1966]. A Colombian nun spoke about him with dignity, we drank bottles of pop and ate a cake in his honour, and stood to invoke and salute him:

Compañero Camillo Torres – ¡Presente, presente, presente!

And then a bonus: some *compas* had brought guitars.

They sang for an hour, and this was something quite different from 'the guitar in arms'. The music was pensive and caressing. The songs were low-key – no strut, strum or thrashing in them, no banging of chords. Long flowing melodic lines carried songs of reflection, songs of wary and very cautious optimism. Facing the ever-more apparent truth – that the Triumph of the People was very hard pressed – they called upon personal love as a source of strength in a dark time when it was no longer possible to say with any honest conviction that victory was assured. They were musically elaborate, often intricately harmonized with drawn-out vocal melismas. They were musician's songs; they certainly demanded more fingering skills than an amateur of the guitar like myself might possess. I liked them, they were fine songs. The singers were Salvador Cardenal – nephew of poet and Minister of Culture Ernesto Cardenal – and his close associate Salvador Bustos. The songs were their own. They were not really songs that others might sing.

In the following days I read a great deal, both the Managua daily press and the offerings of the bookshops. There was not a lot to be seen now of the popular, participatory literature of the masses that had been such a hallmark of the early days. It could not be said exactly that a reaction had set in, but still there was an air of a closing of ranks accompanied by a certain intellectual introspection. In the immediate aftermath of the Triumph the Sandinista leadership, in particular Commandante Bayardo Arce, had declared that the pre-revolutionary culture of the days of General Somoza had been an offensive decadence to which there would be no return. But by 1986 there were not a few minds casting back to the 'high' culture of 'before', and becoming fearful of losing touch with that ancestry.

The pedigree of the revolutionary arts in Nicaragua is long enough, after all. In the historical anthology (state published) of Nicaraguan verse there are fiery denunciations of the Yankee dollar and its vile mercenaries by authors active in the early 19th century. Now there was a call gone out to scholars and academics to re-edit, re-publish and re-appraise that work of the 'national poet' Ruben Dario whose long poem *Azul* was coming up for a centenary. And meanwhile, in the new poems and prose that were being published, there was that same tone that I'd caught in the songs: no longer triumph, but an almost melancholic introspection, a voice saying: We can make it if we try, but what if we don't try hard enough or in the wrong way, or if we are simply wrong? Have we any personal resources and reserves to win us time to rethink the next move?

'I can introduce you to them if you like' said Eric, my host in Managua, meaning the two Salvadors. 'They're a movement, they're *Volcanto.*'

Was that a performing group? No, a movement, as he said – a tendency, an 'eruption of song'. It sounds better in its Spanish pun, *Volcanto.*

And so they came to tea, or rather rum, more readily available in Managua than tea. Eric had given them to understand that I was there writing articles for the British press; unfortunately he hadn't explained that they were mostly articles on public health for *Medicine in Society* and the *Economist Development Report.* I'm afraid the two

Salvadors must have been very disappointed in me; they came to the house with embarrassing swiftness.

'Is this an interview? I've recorded with Jackson Browne, did you know that?'

Yes, so I'd heard.

So we drank rum and ice all afternoon, and they had guitars with them so naturally they played. More of the same songs, very tender, lingering and thoughtful.

I asked, what does *Volcanto* do? Do you make records? This caused Cardenal to peer into his rum. Bustos remarked that getting recorded was a problem now. For musicians of their calibre? (And – though I wasn't drunk enough to say it – for the Minister's nephew?). Oh yes, a problem. A technical one for a start, said Bustos.

'There's one old record press and precious few materials. Hey, how many did they make of your first record?'

Cardenal said it was perhaps two thousand disks.

So *Volcanto* had been recorded?

'No, that was before *Volcanto*. It's not so easy now. It's not so easy to explain either. It's not exactly a popular style, you see. There's not such an audience…'

I wondered what it might be like to be a musician of the first order who, having come through the ordeal by fire singing along with the people only to find that, by singing better and in a more remote key, some discord had occurred, such that people were no longer listening. What if one was a revolutionary artist finding oneself in a rather less than revolutionary elite backwater by mere

39

reason of one's talent? The very thought seemed grossly patronising to the populace and yet those excellent songwriters seemed, well, sad.

We drank more rum, *Flor de Caña,* virtually the only commodity in which the country is self-sufficient; there were litres of it about the house. They sang some more, and then it was my turn. I am not a revolutionary songwriter and I know few revolutionary songs. In fact, all I could think of was 'The Bold Feinian Men' in the playing of which *Flor de Caña* in no way assisted my fingerwork:

Glory O, glory O to the bold Fenian men!

– in a mellow British public school voice. They said nicely that it really was a good song. Or *really,* it *was* a good song. I fetched more ice. By now they were just singing for each other, and to hell with *Time* or *Harpers* or *NME* or whoever I was supposed to write for.

If I would like to come to his house, insisted Cardenal, he would give me all the hard facts I needed for my article, about Jackson Browne and so on. I was vastly flattered but, what with one thing and another, I never got there. I did, however, get to a record shop and bought, for $50 US hard, virtually the entire catalogue of Nicaraguac, the state recording company, fifteen disks at any rate. Very interesting some of them are, especially the *Canto Epico del Frente Sandinista,* a sort of folk opera of the revolution. There's *La Guitarra Armada,* and the early songs of Cardenal, and a lot of *costeño* dance music. There are also the songs of the national literacy campaigns – *Turning the darkness to light* – and a recording (glory O!) of the hymn in praise of bananas.

By Christmas I'd gone east to a more conservative revolutionary culture, an enclave in Burma which (unlike Sandinista Nicaragua) doesn't bulk menacingly on the maps of the Western allies but towards which (also unlike Nicaragua) certain Western allies happily slip a bob or two if they can do so without jeopardising their civil engineering contracts with the supposedly 'socialist' government in Rangoon. That is to say, I spent Christmas in Kawthoolay, the free Karen State that has been slogging it out with the armies of the Burmese government for the last four decades.

The Karen are often counted among the 'hill tribes' of the Burma-Thai border, and in the north of Thailand their villages are subjected to tourists who come to gawk at their quaint and curious idyll, to photograph their funny clothes and to buy their weaving. But whereas the Akha, Lisu and other groups may be numbered in a few tens of thousands, the Karen are numerous; there may be three million or more. In 1948 they rose in revolt, seceding from the new Union of Burma and declaring the Karen Free State of Kawthoolay, which to this day has not been recognised by a single foreign government. With a force of regular troops trained and led initially by ex-British Army Karen officers, they now hold a narrow stretch of hill territory between Burma and Thailand which shrinks each year.

They are hardly the type of fanatics to frighten (or delight) the Pentagon. They fish the rivers and bump up and down in dug-out canoes with noisy outboard motors, they collect bamboo and honey and hunt monkeys in the forest, and cultivate rice on burned hillside fields. They still weave, but for the most part dress in cheap textiles brought in from Thailand and Burma. While the forest dwellers' lives do not change greatly from year to year, the lives of the Delta Karen who come to join the rebel state have changed out of all recognition, and they now struggle to adapt to the life of small riverine forest communities, to be one with their more traditional kin while yet retaining those urban, cosmopolitan skills which they consider vital to the running of an independent state, and of which they are proud. Sophisticated, well educated and for the most part Christian, those who arrived lately in Kawthoolay have families and friends still in Mergui, Tavoy, Moulmein and Rangoon, and they don't know where or how they will ever see them again, or how the low-level but insistent dry-season fighting will end. The village I stayed in was, economically, tightly bound to Thailand, but the people look constantly, longingly towards Burma. Amongst themselves they often talk in Burmese.

I had got to know a man called True Love, who was a soldier and teacher. Ten years ago he'd been a minor civil servant in the Burmese administration, but constantly missed promotion. Persistent small slights and insults from Burman colleagues had worked on him to the point where he was persuaded to throw in his lot with the secessionist state, to which he and a group of friends duly came. True Love had left parents and siblings behind him and, having little opportunity to keep in contact with them, was prey to loneliness. But he met and married a woman from a riverside village and at last found his revolutionary role in the Kawthoolay schools system, as well as being an army sergeant with an M16 in his house.

But he and his friends were also musicians. When True Love informed me that the highlight of the festivities would be a concert, I understood that he himself would be a front-line performer.

Christmas was a pleasure. When I tactlessly asked True Love what he would be giving his wife Silver for Christmas, he replied simply, 'My love' – and that left the clock I'd bought for their bamboo house looking rather vulgar. The village was central to the district and had a large school – almost 300 pupils, most of them refugees – and much of the fun was focused there. The Education Department, having nothing festive to give the children, at least tried to make the day memorable by organising a feast. But, in fact, there were gifts; a European charity had decided that it would donate school supplies for the coming year. An Englishwoman who was visiting at the time had given money to buy sweets and biscuits and we spent half the night putting these into paper bags labelled *Jesus loves you.* On Christmas morning all the school benches were brought out into the open in front of the main classroom block, and formed into a wide semi-circle with tables at its centre. They'd made a Christmas tree of bamboo and wire wrapped in green and red crepe, which looked decidedly more cheerful than the school building. There'd been an air raid sometime ago during which one building had been hit. There had been two casualties, both of them ducks; also, a tin of cooking oil had been punctured, which answered the question of what to do with the ducks. But, fearful for their children, the Karen had dispersed the school buildings and painted the biggest in camouflage drab.

There, on the tables by the tree, all the goodies were heaped. The children assembled, sang a creed of youth, then recited the four principles of Ba U Gyi, Kawthoolay's founder:

- For us, surrender is out of the question

- Recognition of the Karen state must be completed

- We shall retain our arms

- We shall determine our own destiny

After which, class by class, they stepped crisply forward, all in blue and white uniforms, and received their packets of pencils, their exercise and colouring books, and their paper bags of custard creams. True Love took their photos; it was a solemn moment.

Not so the school feast; this was inspired gaiety. Each class had planned and cooked its own menu, scrounging a chicken here, some noodles there, even putting a few *Baht* together to send out to Thailand for some little jellies in plastic tubs. The teachers were not supposed to help, although poor Silver, in charge of the kindergarten, had little choice. When the hour came, the tables spread out beneath the trees were heaped for the feast; on some tacit signal, all the teachers (with myself and the English woman donor in tow) descended on each table in turn like Elizabeth Tudor and her court on progress, moving on to another class to eat with them, with shrieks and hoots and giggles, the children rushing to and fro to see what each other had cooked, the little jellies popping gaily out of their pots, infinite good humour, cheerful singing, warm-heartedness, delight and broad smiles spread from ear to ear of the broad Karen faces about me. I've seldom enjoyed a Christmas dinner quite like that. Nor, it seemed had they. Another Karen soldier/teacher, beaming upon the scene, invoked with happy contempt the name of the [then] Burmese military ruler who numbered economic strangulation amongst his tactics against Kawthoolay:

'If Ne Win could see us now, he would cry, he would cry!'

But it was the Karen New Year Variety Concert that I remember most vividly. They'd been preparing for days beforehand. Under the guidance of one very young teacher who knew the steps, they learned the Bamboo Dance in which the dancers have to skip through a grid of twelve large bamboo poles slammed together rhythmically, snapping at the dancers' ankles. They'd rehearsed the Rice Planting dance in which files of boys and girls wind in and out

44

of each other while some mime the making of seed holes with bamboo staves and others dab their feet into the centre to press the seedlings in. And they'd learned an elaborate dance in which the lines of dancers swung about to form letters, spelling out whatever word you wished. They were tricky, complex dances; the practices went on hour after hour on hot afternoons, out in the open by the kitchens or in the shade behind the church. They went on into the evenings by the light of a neon strip over the kitchen door, words and rhythms somewhat fouled by the noise of the generator, the dust cloud from the feet and the clapping bamboos sapping the thin light of the neon.

There was a stage; True Love – who seemed to have the unofficial role of entertainments supervisor – directed its building. It was all of bamboo, with a drawing curtain and some Christmas tinsel, and electric light from another generator in the trees behind. The Christmas tree was there on stage, as was a quantity of electric amplification.

'Who,' I asked, 'bought all that lot?'

'The Education Department; it was second-hand. We have two or three groups that play. We made a tape.'

Karen New Year's Day began in a slightly damp fashion. At an early hour, two unfamiliar sounds called me from my hammock to the parade ground. One was a large bronze drum – Kawthoolay's national emblem. These drums were made in South-East Asia for perhaps two millennia, and many villages still have one. They feature little cast frogs hopping together around the sounding face; these, in Karen interpretation, signify the unity of the people. On the side of the drum there's an elephant running away from the unified frogs, and close inspection reveals a little lump of bronze on the surface just behind the elephant: it has shat itself in fear. This, obviously, is the Burmese Army running away. No one knew exactly how old our bronze drum was, but it lived in the school and was brought out to be beaten at Karen New Year. The other sound was a small, high-pitched cow-horn bugle – a Karen battle trumpet, said to chill the hearts of Burmese soldiers.

It was chill enough already. A heavy, dark mist lay over the parade ground. Hills, houses, clumps of bamboo poked up, baseless, over the thick and un-tropical grey. Small groups of villagers and soldiers assembled near the drum, while the governing class formed up in a phalanx opposite. In double file the schoolchildren came, the luckier ones in nylon jackets over their thin uniforms. The flag was run up, the anthem sung; the Colonel made a speech. And then we all went and had breakfast together on long bamboo tables under the trees by the District Judge's house: rice, and pork (very fat) and chilli sauce. For much of the rest of that day they played sports – volleyball, football, wheelbarrow races, and tug o'war – 'Very old Karen game, Jo, you'll not have seen this before' – all organised by a jocular young teacher in military uniform by the name of Nixon ('I was born the day that man was elected. My father thought it must be auspicious').

Meanwhile, behind the bright blue church, the dance practice continued; the bamboo poles were pounded on the ground for three beats before snapping at the dancers' ankles on the fourth – *thump, thump, thump, clack!* – with little puffs of talcum-fine dust whisping up from their toes as they skipped across the grid. They were not getting it right. True Love strummed it out on his guitar as the young teacher sang the words from her exercise book:

> Now we've reached the mountains, we see the lovely scenery.
> This is our heritage. The fields and villages are all Karen.

46

They are poor, they pray for education to release them.
Karen people, duty and kin call you: come and help them!

'That,' I observed rather belligerently to True Love, 'is not very traditional. At least, the tune may be, but the words are obviously revolutionary. Do these young people actually know the traditional dances?'

He riposted: 'Here you see them dancing a traditional dance.'

'But there is only one teacher who knows how to do it.'

'That's our Karen way. Our dance troupes always have an instructor who knows the traditions.'

'But many of these are Delta Karen, city kids for whom these dances aren't really part of the heritage at all.'

'No, Jo, that's not right. In all the towns in Burma where there are Karen we know these dances. We do them!'

'When?'

'At Karen New Year, all in Karen costume.'

'The Burmese government allows that?'

'We must thank the British administration, which gazetted the Karen New Year as a public holiday. Ne Win would not dare reverse it.'

There being little enough that the Karen do thank the British for now, I settled for this.

The concert began with speeches, as official programmes do anywhere. The PA was prone to feedback, the generator to stalling – neither of these Karen monopolies either. The villagers gathered in front of the bamboo stage, small children cross-legged on the dirt up front, their elders on all the wooden church benches brought out into the open. In the background, by the white light of pressure lamps or the smoking flame of naked wicks stuck into cans filled with paraffin, women sold chicken soup and noodles and rice-flour fritters, and Burmese cigars.

'You want to be careful with those cigars. Feel them carefully, weigh them in your hand.'

'Why?'

'Sometimes they pack a .22 bullet inside, pointing backwards.'

In the darkness, one occasionally bumped into a figure in camouflage green hugging a carbine or a Kalashnikov. Very rarely, I glimpsed a courting couple pecking nervously at each other in the shadows. Karen morality is famously stern. Traditionally, public demonstrations of affection were strictly limited to certain occasions: one did one's spooning at funerals.

After the speeches, after the sports prize-giving, a special item: Homage to the Elders. There were four of them, three women and a man, and to a Karen version of 'Silver Threads among the Gold' they were led onto the stage by girls in maiden's dress, a white shift with high bust and delicate scarlet stripes. Each Elder was presented with a rose, red for three of them, and white for the lady in her eighties. Then they each received a box containing a Thai sponge cake smothered in foaming *ersatz* cream.

And then the dancing. A dozen boys and girls in red and white were gathered behind the stage. It is obvious that Karen traditional dance is intended for daylight and a hard, stamped ground between the houses, not the springy confinement of a bamboo platform.

48

They managed; the grid dance had to be scaled down to eight poles but they got through it with ankles unbruised. The planting dance was hampered by the lights – two brilliant incandescent bulbs that blazed from the front – while True Love strummed out the gentle tune on the guitar with a steady rhythm and the young teacher sang it once again:

> Saw Ter Kwa, O my beloved,
> Just as Ku Naw Lay loved Naw Muh Eh,
> Plucking her from the serpent's jaws,
> Just so, I say, I'll love only you.

I happen to know that in the folk tale referred to here both lovers come to a sticky end, Ku Naw Lay cutting his own throat to bribe the serpent to relinquish his bride who jumped onto his funeral pyre.

Then came the spelling dance in which the flowing lines of dancers, red and white, spelled out 'KAREN NEW YEAR'.

It was time for the revolutionary rock. It was the Rangoon lads, soldiers, teachers and pop stars, four of them onstage with drum kit and guitars, but for this community event just as a backing band while, one after another, the vocalists came forward, children mostly, still in their blue and white school uniforms, one song each extolling duty, or love of the hills, forests and rivers of Kawthoolay. The songs shared a common rhythm and a rather limited melodic pattern. It was only too clear where the roots of Karen *nueva cançion* lay: it was Country & Western of the most liberally sugared variety. 'Country Roads,' 'Nobody's Child' – these were just below the surface.

'That's the sort of music we like,' said True Love. 'And what are you going to play for us?'

I?

49

'Now, as a special event, a solo from Mr Jo.'

The last time I had sung on a bamboo stage had been Java, seven years ago, when the stage had wobbled so much that the microphone had fallen over.

'True Love, what should I sing?'

'Something about revolution '

I said I'd do 'The Bold Fenian Men' and asked him to translate a summary for the audience: 'This is about some brave Irishmen who fought to make their country free.'

'What happened?

'It… took a long time.'

'Free from whom?'

'Us. The British.'

It was perhaps not the most tactful choice of song.

> … and wise men have told us their cause was a failure.
> We may have brave men, but we'll never have better.
> Glory O, glory O to the bold Fenian men.

Now the schoolgirls sang again to the crowd invisible in the dark middle ground between the stage lamps and the smoking lamps of the noodle and cigar vendors. They sang of Burmese oppression, of villages burned and crops destroyed, of violent interrogation and forced porterage of ammunition.

Afterwards, there was a midnight church service and then a special treat. An 18-inch television was placed on the front of the stage. It had grown rather cold and the thick, heavy mist was settling down into the river valley again. The crowd packed tighter towards the little screen, pulled their jackets tighter against the chill, tugged woollen balaclavas over their heads and settled down to watch *The Battle of the Bulge.*

I asked True Love for a copy of the tape he and the lads had made. I'd expected an amateurish discordant racket caught on someone's ghetto-blaster, but I was wrong again: decent recording equipment had been borrowed. The tape was a slick production of songs by several hands. There are, of course, hymns to the natural beauty of Kawthoolay; there's a commemoration of the day in 1950 when Ba U Gyi, founder of their Free State, had been gunned down in an ambush (like Michael Collins); there were songs of hope and of courage, of Karen soldiers called away from sweethearts to the front line. True Love's best known is called 'Love & Duty':

> I love you, Karen girl, your beauty and sweet voice.
> I hope to see you one day soon – that will be wonderful.
> When I return from the front line,
> I hope to see your welcoming smile.

The song hit its mark; many people, especially the soldiers for whom it was intended, could sing it. The tape comes smartly packaged with a crisply printed coloured sleeve. It's called *Ta Kee Suh Ta Ker Paw* – like Nicaraguan literacy songs: 'From darkness to light.'

Before I left, True Love asked me to record 'The Bold Fenian Men' onto a cassette for him so that he could learn it. His wife's granny was there, a humorous old lady with a mouth full of crimson betel. She enjoyed the tune. Re-playing the tape, a most unexpected accompaniment could be heard: a Karen grandmother in the forest singing the refrain of an Irish revolutionary song, over and over:

> Glory O! Glory O! Glory O!

ONLY THE SONS OF SHADOW FEAR THE LIGHT

At four a.m. a polite but anxious scrabble began for seats on the flight from Belem at the mouth of the Amazon to the forest town of Altamira. No one had foreseen it; the meeting of Indians and concerned parties, called by Kayapo chief Paulinho Paikan and the Union of Indigenous Nations, had suddenly become the front line of world ecological warfare. Anthropologists and MPs, environmentalists, doctors, industrialists, trade unionists, scientists, two hundred reporters and a dozen film crews from four continents inundated the frontier town on the banks of the Xingu River to hear the Kayapo and their allies denounce flooding of the rainforest by hydroelectric dams.

At Altamira, visitors were three to a room except for Granada TV who stayed in the Kiss Me Motel (rooms there normally by the hour). Outside, a war of slogans. Local traders, keen for the business that would accompany the dam, had slung banners down the main street. *Energy is the lungs of the world!* said one, twisting an old conservationist cliché. *Hydroelectricity is the light at the end of the tunnel!*

Dams are ecological AIDS! retorted the green graffiti. But the local Democratic Rural Union (UDR), an alliance of agribusiness interests, hit back below the Indians' belt: *Only the sons of shadow fear the light.*

In the shade of trees around a Catholic church retreat five miles away, 800 Indians had built their camp with hammocks in the cloisters and simple thatched shelters outside. Armed guards – Indian and police – stood at the gate; shots had been fired into the camp at night, and besides, the Indians needed some relief from the film cameras. Visiting hours for outsiders were strict; the camp was a treasured achievement. It had taken months of negotiation by Paikan, Kune-i and others to persuade rival tribes to come together, and an arduous speaking tour of Europe and Canada by the two leaders and an anthropologist, Darrel Posey, to raise funds and interest. On their return, all three had been arraigned by the courts for un-Brazilian activities – though the charge appears to have been dropped in a blur of official embarrassment.

On Monday morning, the Kayapo and Xavante danced in lines and clusters of men with bodies painted black and red, bright green macaw feather head-dresses and slender wooden clubs topped with a short point for stubbing into faces. The cameras mixed in and clung to them, and the wits said that serious ecological harm must result from the expense of photographic silver and gelatine at Altamira. The Kayapo, now the vanguard of Indian resurgence, have video cameras of their own, and it was possible to photograph a European journalist snapping a Kayapo who was in turn filming a Japanese who was focussing on an Indian mother and baby under a tree.

Each morning at eight, buses brought us to a vast, ugly cement sports hall with a dais of desks and microphones. Each Indian group came in at the trot, chanting, then sat quietly on palm leaves all day beside other tribes who have for centuries been their customary rivals. Today they have more ruthless enemies, and some warriors stood ready with taut bows and two metre arrows.

'Those might have been ceremonial once,' said an anthropologist beside me. 'Now can you see the tips glinting?' Around the Indians, a protective ring of young white Brazilian activists stood holding hands – a not entirely happy symbol.

We listened to five days of rhetoric: 'This is a battle for all mankind. We are here to witness the last great struggle for our planet's genetic resources. We demand, and we deserve, full legal protection of our lives and our lands. We are as much Brazilian as anyone!' A British film director complained that this was Seventies slogan politics, barely worth listening to. But delicate nerves were being touched, not least Brazilian nationalism. There have been few more bitter arguments in recent Brazilian politics: are not the Indians – and the church and others backing them – obstructing national development, in the pay of some fictitious Christian Church World Council or other malicious foreigners?

The UDR painted a slogan on the wall: *We welcome the Indigenous Peoples. We hope you do not feel used by un-patriotic interests.*

Others were blunter: *Go home, gringos. Where are your Indians now?*

Inept conservationists sometimes demand that the Amazon basin be 'internationalised' or bought in exchange for Brazil's foreign debt. President Sarney retorts furiously that not an inch of forest will be sold into foreign hands (blithely ignoring the enormous control already exercised by transnationals and foreign banks). But at Altamira the Indians assure everyone else: 'We are all Brazilians, good Brazilians. The land is ours, as Brazilian citizens.'

There is, however, as much variety of outlook and economic interest among the Indians as there is among white Brazilians. Some are loath to emerge from the forest; they shun contact, speak no Portuguese, seek no material wealth. Other Indians are doing very nicely out of modern Brazil; still more would like to. Pombo was at Altamira, a powerful man who has made his fortune out of selling off the forest for lumber, and who is famous for his epicurean lifestyle. Such men stand to profit, at least financially, from the boom that will accompany the Kararao dam.

Nor is the situation of every tribe the same. The fourteen Kayapo tribes are surviving relatively well. Their numbers are increasing and, by enforcing a toll on gold mined in their area, they've gained a substantial dollar income enabling them to buy an aircraft to patrol their lands and short-wave radio to link their villages. The Xavante now live on a reservation; other smaller tribes face extinction. The numerous (20,000) and disparate Yanomami are being killed off by the gold prospectors who have swarmed into their territory. Paulinho Paiakan brought all these interests together at Altamira.

Out in the streets, other citizens were showing their hand. The pro-dam movement, MOPROK, staged a rally; it had no style, but some impact. A thousand local traders, farmers and their followers paraded with placards on trucks, road-graders and motorcycles. Pretty farmer's daughters, looking too demur to weed a window box, rode through town on horseback proclaiming the tons of cocoa they'd harvested this year. The Indians wisely stayed in their camp, and a potentially nasty afternoon passed off in good humour, if not exactly quietly.

The next morning, however, there was violence of a rhetorical sort. The engineering director of Eletronorte – the power company responsible for the hydroelectric scheme – sat on the dais to take the flak from Indians and environmentalists, and from Paiakan in the chair.

'There's nothing hasty about this,' said the Director. 'We've been planning Kararao for five years.'

'Then,' said Paiakan, 'you should have consulted us five years ago.'

'These dams are a credit to Brazilian engineering.'

'But for Brazil they have been disastrous.'

A Kayapo woman got up from the floor. Her words were drowned in the roar of camera shutters but her gesture was eloquent: she stroked the Director's cheeks and neck with a machete.

'Not to worry,' announced Paiakan, eyeing the armed police by the door. 'This is a traditional rhetorical gesture. We cannot be bound by your conventions. We must speak in our own way.'

The Director kept his nerve, but then peevishly announced that the Indian name for the site of the dam, Kararao, was to be dropped and the Portuguese Belo Monte used instead.

'Kararao will always be Kararao to us,' said Paiakan. 'Do you know what it means? It's a war cry.' At which, three hundred Kayapo Indians stood and let the Director hear what they meant by a war cry.

'It is a war,' said Brazilian ecologist Jose Lutzemberger to a circle of journalists. 'And we will all suffer. The earth's climate will undoubtedly change, though we cannot know how much until it happens. But if there's another ice-age, I'd rather be Brazilian. Last time there was still tropical forest in Brazil when northern Europe was under a kilometre of ice.'

'Doesn't the government listen to you?' someone asked.

'What more evidence do they need?' replied Lutzemberger. 'Last year, smoke from deliberate fires in the Brazilian Amazon closed the airport at La Paz, Bolivia. There are only two sorts of people in this government: those who don't care and those who are, frankly, too stupid.'

Other celebrities spoke up. Tam Dalyell the Scottish parliamentarian told the hall that he'd apply screws to the British government and the World Bank, and that what Brazil needed was nuclear power. The Belgian Greens, the Italian Friends of the Earth, a Brazilian film star all harangued us. Rumours of Brigitte Bardot and Jane Fonda came to nothing, but Sting appeared at the Indian campsite arm in arm with Chief Raoni, promoting a controversial scheme for a Brazilian foundation with foreign funds to buy the forest, thus side-stepping the 'patriots' but leading some to ask why land should be paid for which is supposed to be the Indians' right and property anyway. The Pope sent a message of support, as did the Italian government. Indigenous leaders from Canada and from the USA came to the platform. Over and above them all, one man remained the star of the proceedings: the instigator of this and previous actions, the unflappable, painted and feathered chairman of the week's proceedings, Paulinho Paiakan now had the status of a world leader of the international conservation movement.

Outside the hall, opinion remained divided. Altamira, former one-horse town, now has an all-weather airstrip, metalled roads, telex, TV and radio stations, private clinics and half a dozen supermarkets of a size that would not disgrace an English provincial town. To one side is the Trans-Amazon highway; to the other, the mile-wide Xingu River. Altamira claims to have quadrupled its population in a decade, making it the fastest growing town in Brazil. But in the whole municipality (an area slightly larger than West Germany) there are not much more than 120,000 people; twenty thousand dam construction workers and their families would make a difference. Fortunes might well be made.

So to find any local support for the Indians was unexpected. A young woman sewing and selling clothes in her own small shop was adamantly opposed to the dam, but feared she was in a minority. Indeed; in a backstreet, Antonio Soares da Costa, chairman of the local Construction Workers Union, dragged us into his small wooden office for some hard truths.

'What I want to know first is, who's paying for all you people to come here? Where do all the airfares come from? If you gave the cash to Altamira instead, we wouldn't need the dam! Look, do you know how many Indians will be displaced by Kararao? Three hundred and sixty. There may be two hundred times that number living in this town alone. Why do we want power? Because we have serious problems. We have extremely expensive diesel-generated electricity, we have high infant mortality, poor hospitals, few schools, dreadful roads. We want development and prosperity like you, like anybody. We don't want to live in jungle misery.'

Which would not have impressed the Xavante leader in the hall, who was saying: We are not a poor, miserable people. We are proud, and in our own way we are very rich. Altamira is a slum, and if the people here think that just by growing fast it will become any less of a slum, they are deluded.

It was not only about dams. David Yanomami described the invasion of Yanomami lands and the slaughter of his people by gold prospectors. Scientists told of mercury from the mines polluting the Amazon basin. Others denounced the absurd economics of cattle ranching. Representative of Brazil's multifarious urban and rural poor spoke of their working lives and of the desperate need for land and labour reform, for solidarity among the oppressed. Messages of support arrived from two dozen unions, including metalworkers, priests, landless labourers and doctors.

'Anyone who says we're not Brazilians,' said a union delegate, 'is discounting half of Brazilian society.'

On Friday a joint communiqué was issued by the Union of Indigenous Nations and their supporters, condemning forest destruction and announcing that they'd be seeking a court injunction against the dam. Prizes were distributed. The memory of Chico Mendes [a murdered environmentalist] was saluted. The Kayapo – all warring groups together – performed a last ceremony on the football pitch, invisible to the spectators because of the dense wall of media cameras surrounding them. Certain eco-groupies made cash offers for their headdresses. The Board of Eletronorte issued a statement, that they would not meet with any more Indians unless they were guaranteed freedom from women with machetes. The journalists began to jostle for flights out of Altamira. Twenty-four hours after the end of the meeting, local Rotarians had replaced some of the banners with new ones announcing the contest for 'Miss Altamira 1989'.

THE POCKET TRUE LOVE

1. COLONEL MARVEL

Down the long spine of hills that divides Burma from Thailand lies a string of rebel enclaves in revolt against the Burmese government. These are the hill tribe armies: Kachin, Karen, Wa and Shan. Here, in bamboo and timber huts in the rain forest, is all the machinery of free government: schools, hospitals, Departments of Forestry, Transport and Trade. Their fortunes rise and fall, their tiny treasuries are empty, their ragtag armies swept aside by battalions of Burmese regulars blundering towards them through the undergrowth. But, against all predictions, somehow they persist. Some have been fighting for more than forty years.

I spent an illegal year in the Burmese jungle, training young Karen as paramedics. We lived in an overgrown village by a muddy river, in the most malarial forest in the world. The landscape is a wild confusion of ridges, crowned by magnificent hardwood trees, draped with orchids and lianas, cluttered with bamboos and ferns. Part of the year is very dry, and fires march through the undergrowth in long lines up the slopes like relentless grouse beaters. Then, when the rains return, the river boils, the bamboo shoots upward, the air teems with mosquitoes and the mud crawls with six-inch centipedes and black scorpions, eight inches long, like small lobsters in the jungle.

Our local rebel military commander was called Colonel Marvel. He was a stout, balding man of some sixty years. In 1944 he had been trained as a mechanic by the Japanese, but had then fought for the British. In 1950 he joined the rebels of the Karen National Union fighting for autonomy. During forty years of jungle warfare, he saw the Karen leadership split and split again, faction turning on faction, Communists giving way to Baptists, appealing first to Mao Zedong and then to Mrs Thatcher for support, and receiving no reply.

Colonel Marvel had been assigned to our District at a time when the war was being fought elsewhere. The Colonel was a sick man. He was diabetic and overweight, his kidneys were failing; he'd been relieved of front line command for a rest. But I began to see other reasons for his transfer. Impetuous decisions, frantic activity and contradictory orders were not the way to defeat the Burmese.

Resting was the least of Colonel Marvel's talents. His forest house was certainly not restful. It crawled with scorpions, which skulked in gaps between the timbers by my bed; I drove them deeper by frying their tails with my cigarette lighter. The house was lit by neon tubes without switches; they came on with the village generator at 6pm, went off at nine and on again before dawn. The Colonel needed to be up and about. There were soldiers to train, schools and hospitals to build, and a new scheme for trading bamboos for bullets across the Thai border. He was only still and quiet if reading the *Bangkok Post* and chortling over the antics of Mrs Thatcher, or if lying prostrate having his calves massaged by the wife of the Forestry Officer.

The Colonel drove himself through the forest in a pickup with *Colonel Marvel* in silvered plastic letters on the dashboard. One day he'd wear smart green fatigues, the next a silver-grey jump suit. He would have been Burma's best dressed insurgent were it not for the blue towel that he carried round his neck to catch the sweat. He would scurry about issuing commands. One day, we were all told to dig air raid shelters. But the shelters filled with rain.

61

'We shan't be shot,' wailed my neighbours, 'we'll simply drown!'

When Colonel Marvel had gone, the shelters were converted into latrines.

He interfered with everything, reorganising the hospital and schools, the Forestry Department and Women's Organisation, sacking everybody and appointing himself to do it all. The village gossips were incensed:

'He knows nothing about Health. And he has no time! What about the Army, and Finance and Communications and everything else he meddles with?'

So the village bickered, while Moses the Pastor prayed that they'd all come to their senses and remember the common cause – because now the Burmese Army was pressing through the forest towards us.

But the Colonel's confrontations with his staff continued. I saw him in a spectacular fury one afternoon. Some pet scheme had gone wrong. He let off steam by washing his new pickup – which the Finance Department had not very privately called a gross waste of scarce funds. There, among the wood and bamboo huts, the radio shack and the air-raid shelters, the Colonel roared abuse at miserable youths who'd left smudges on the chrome. His staff fussed about, enthusiastically agreeing with everything he spat out about refugees, inadequate officers, foreigners and other incompetents by whom he was surrounded. Behind the sycophancy in the officers' faces, I saw exasperation writ large. What did the Colonel expect, if he issued a dozen contradictory orders?

He took me to a Karen refugee camp. There were problems. Burmese campaigns had pushed more refugees into Karen territory. The people were sick, there was little water, security was lax, rice reserves low, the garrison needed a shake-up and the school an inspection. The Colonel thought he could sort it all out in five days. After a long journey south, I sank exhausted into my hammock.

But not the Colonel. He summoned the local staff to the command hut and spent the evening drawing charts of the revolutionary hierarchy. The next morning, he began work at five, sending officials hurrying away with new instructions. He inspected the militia, a ferocious bunch dressed in sarongs and flip-flops. I have a photograph of the Colonel that day teaching a twelve year-old boy how to fire a carbine.

On Revolution Day, I heard him exhorting his people to greater efforts.

'Thirty nine years ago, when the Karen took up arms for freedom, I was there. I was young and vigorous then; today I am an old man. But my belief in our future has not dimmed one bit.'

One day, a legal document arrived for me from the UK. It needed signing, and a witness. I meant to ask the Colonel to oblige, and I imagined his entry:

Name: Colonel Marvel. *Occupation:* Insurgent.

But then I doubted: if your nation doesn't legally exist, can you be a legal witness? So I asked someone in Thailand instead. I have always regretted this.

2. HARVEST MOON

The headquarters village of the Karen rebels lay on flat ground in a bend of the river, surrounded by thickly forested Burmese hills. The forest was our protection: the Karen people were natural foresters, perfectly at ease in the jungle – but the Burmese army hated it. Our greatest danger came from the air. Many of the houses had tin roofs which were dangerously visible. I noticed that the Karen often painted theirs dark green. When they built my house, the new tin shone brilliantly, a fine target for the Burmese air force.

Many of the leaders of the rebellion were educated people come from the cities of Burma to join the rebel forces in the hills. Here, they met and mixed with forest Karen, among whom the old traditions were still strong. Our Headquarters village was not like a traditional Karen village at all. It was divided into distinct areas for health workers, teachers, or Karen National Liberation Army soldiers. There were neat paths and vegetable plots with bamboo fences, banana palms and pawpaw trees, and pumpkin vines growing over the houses. Nails and timber were provided by the authorities, but everyone built their own home, raised on stilts off the monsoon mud and away from the snakes, scorpions and poisonous centipedes that crawled in it. They had walls of split and flattened bamboo, a double layer to stop the tropical rains driving through and soaking your bedding. We also had a hospital, a school, a big Baptist church painted blue, and a jail of small huts with a neat flowerbed outside the gates where the flowers spelt the English word, JAIL.

But, alongside the muddy brown river and shaded by tall kapok trees, there was one row of houses larger and grander than the rest. I called this Millionaires Row. These buildings were of heavy timbers, with real wooden floors – though traditional Karen were content to sit on bamboo flooring. These houses had broad verandahs, even tables where senior rebel officials would sit smoking rough Burmese cigars and chewing betel, spitting out the juice so that the floorboards were stained blood red. These were the homes of the chief of health, the head of education – and Harvest Moon, the District Justice.

Harvest Moon was a massively built old man with a huge belly who always wore a white shirt and a sarong. He was kindly, with a keen sense of humour; he once told me how he'd met a black panther on a jungle path. 'I pointed my umbrella at it like a rifle – and then we both ran away.'

Someone told me, 'Actually, Harvest Moon was once a drunken sailor.' But now he personified the Law. He'd put his wild youth behind him, and had a fine big house and family. These days, he was very dignified and senior.

One day Harvest Moon exchanged houses with his neighbour. The reason was curious – and taught me the power of the old traditions among the Karen.

Harvest Moon had two daughters. The eldest, Laura, was something rare and precious in the rebel state: she was a qualified nurse. She'd qualified at a Burmese college before joining the rebellion. It was no surprise when she married Golden Horn, a fast-rising young administrator. He was no traditionalist. I first met him at a rebel army camp deep in the forest near the front line, wearing a floral Hawaiian shirt, several rings and gold-rimmed spectacles. When he married he did not move into his father-in-law's house in the traditional way, but built a bigger house next door, decidedly grander than the old Justice's.

This caused more than a few raised eyebrows. The couple soon had a first baby.

One evening, Laura was sitting with her baby talking to her cousin Shelley. The paraffin lamp was burning low; Shelley fetched the can to refill it, not bothering to extinguish the lamp. He bent over to pour in the paraffin. But the can he had picked up did not contain paraffin: a moment later, all three had terrible burns from a petrol explosion. They were taken by pick-up truck three hours on a dirt track through the forest, out to hospital in Thailand. Shelley, though badly scarred, survived. But Laura and the baby died.

They were buried in a little cemetery there in Millionaires Row, with cement tombstones painted blue and a bamboo fence. The village children hated the tombs. But, when Golden Horn had recovered from the loss of his wife and baby, he married her younger sister.

In Karen tradition, it is very unusual for a widower to remarry for fear of *chai*, terrible events that result from breaking the rules. Perhaps Golden Horn felt that he'd suffered enough bad luck already. Or perhaps he refused to believe in such old-fashioned nonsense.

But it was not to be shaken off. When the second daughter moved across from Harvest Moon's house to Golden Horn's bigger, grander house next door, she felt most uncomfortable. Not only were the tombs of her sister and the baby in front of her; she found that all Laura's possessions were still there in the bedroom.

Something had to change. People said that Golden Horn had offended the spirits, that terrible *chai* would result. Worse, they pointed out that young Golden Horn's house was both grander and – even worse – higher than his respected father in law's home. It was not right at all, the spirits would not accept it. The new bride felt herself doomed, and demanded that something be done. So they exchanged: Golden Horn was forced to give up his fine big house to the Justice, moving into the Justice's old house and dropping back below his level, in every sense.

Many senior rebels were dismayed to think that the old superstitions still ruled their lives; they were proud of their modernity and their Christianity. When I asked why the families had swapped houses, they would only say, 'it is more convenient.' I only learned the real story by chance.

3. BARTHOLOMEW

In my year as a paramedic with the Karen rebels in Burma, my boss and mentor was an elderly man whose own medical skills were largely home-grown, whose teeth were stained red from chewing betel, and whose legs from waist to knee were covered in intricate swirls of tattoo.

His name was Bartholomew. Back in the 1940s, before the British left Burma, Bartholomew had trained as a dresser in a mission hospital. This qualified him to head our local Health Department, which consisted of a handful of nurses, a small hospital which he had largely built with his own hands, a tiny supply of drugs and a dug-out canoe with an outboard motor in which we toured the rebel villages along the river.

Bartholomew had joined the rebellion at the outset, forty years before. He'd been at the epic six-day battle of Myawaddy and personally knew all the Karen leaders. They honoured and deferred to him, but they always called him 'a simple man'. There was nothing simple about his skills, though.

He made me an iron-bladed chopper, whittling a hard cane handle and weaving three delicate little basketwork bands to hold it tight. I watched him thatch houses, lash down bamboo floors and walls, gather medicinal leaves in the forest and grind them into ointments, repair boats, cultivate fruit gardens and raise goats. If a villager stepped on a Burmese landmine, Bartholomew could do a decent amputation. The Karen had so few supplies that they had to be constantly inventive. If a soldier was badly wounded and losing blood, they would cut a fresh coconut, thrust a needle into it and a line into the victim's arm and give him an infusion of coconut juice. They swore that it was sterile and worked very well.

I lived in his house, a tall structure on high wooden posts with a tin roof and a bamboo floor. Here, an ever-varying number of children and relations crowded in, sleeping on, under or around the table in the smoky back kitchen for warmth. There was no privacy whatever. I slung my hammock between two posts by an old poster of the King of Thailand. A *tokay* lizard lived behind this poster, a big speckled monster that did me no harm except deprive me of sleep. At two or three a.m. it would puff itself full of air with mechanical clucks to announce to its girlfriends that something splendid was coming. Then, after an excruciating pause, it would unleash resonant nasal blasts crying *to-kay! to-kay!* With each blast, the King of Thailand swayed back and forth. If I thrashed at the poster to drive it off, the lizard stomped away over the tin roof making an even worse din.

The house was a chaos of doing and making, cooking and repairing. The elder girls slung hammocks in the shade underneath along with the pigs, dogs and chickens, and embroidered pillows with old Mission pieties: *God bless this home* or *Jesus with me now*. Bartholomew's daughter Fragrance made me one. It had crimped borders trimmed with green lace, red roses amid green bows, and a portrait of me as a purple dinosaur playing a yellow guitar. The smaller children went fishing in the muddy river, or carried water, weeded the rice garden or tended the goats. Bartholomew's wife Vermilion sat combing out her yard-long hair and planning trading trips downriver to sell chocolate biscuits, torch batteries, soap powder and antibiotics bought in from Thailand.

Bartholomew himself returned from a river trip with an orphaned baby goat. It was black, very small and unsteady on its feet. To make matters worse, it couldn't cope with the widely spaced bamboo slats of the house floor. Its little feet would slip down between them.

69

Sometimes all four feet would go down together, and the kid would be helpless, its hoofs dangling below the house, while it bleated hysterically. Bartholomew went out and picked it tender young leaves from the forest and fed it these with milk, but it slowly weakened and soon died.

In the evenings, Bartholomew would crouch over his lists of desperately sick refugees from the fighting, his dwindling budget, or his plans for a new training course for village nurses. As he did so, he would hoik his sarong up around his middle, and I could admire his swirling spiral tattoos.

'What do the marks mean?' I asked him.

'They mean that I'm beautiful,' he said.

'Did it hurt?'

'For days.'

'Did your wife think it beautiful?"

"I didn't see that before we got married,' called Vermilion.

'She's lying,' said Bartholomew.

'How old were you?' I asked.

'Thirteen – and out looking for girls.'

Traditionally, the tattoos gave a Karen virility and potency. Today, however, the young rebel soldiers had different symbols. I saw the badge of the Karen National Liberation Army tattooed onto forearms; there was no going back to civilian life in Burma for a young man marked like that.

To organise civilian health care in the face of war is an endless, despairing task. No sooner had Bartholomew built a small clinic, or trained some village girls in basic nursing, than the Burmese attacked, destroyed everything and scattered his staff. The Army interfered endlessly with his work, and they appointed Colonel Marvel's son to run the hospital. This charming young man was a wild hypochondriac, which the villagers said made him an obvious choice for Director: believing that he had all possible diseases himself, he had no trouble in recognising them in others. He quickly squandered all our precious reserves of medicines. He made Bartholomew's life impossible, and I saw the old man reduced to tears of frustration.

But Bartholomew never gave up. Our roving clinics in the villages had as much symbolic value as anything. We were the outward sign of the rebellion caring for its people. We did some good, perhaps; everyone had malaria, and we treated countless cases. I never doubted that the Karen of the forest villages loved and respected Bartholomew. He would put on his plastic flip-flops and his straw hat, take a shoulder bag of medicines and set off along narrow paths calling at every house in the name of the Karen Revolution:

'Is anyone at home? It's Bartholomew. Is anyone sick?' The answer was always: Yes.

4. TRUE LOVE IN LOVE

True Love was the real name (translated) of my closest friend among the Karen rebels. He was not a farmer or a forest tribesman, but had come from the city of Mergui. He was 32, slim, handsome and well–groomed. He hardly looked like an unsophisticated tribesman but, when occasion demanded, he would wear the traditional homespun red shirt with fringes, and a dark red sarong woven on the looms of the rebel Karen National Union.

He was hardly more at home in the forest than I. He'd been a high school student – but he'd seen the prejudice and insults that the Karen people faced every day in Burma. At last, he'd contacted the Karen National Union and made his way with friends up into the hills to join the rebellion.

'You can't imagine,' he said, 'how difficult it is when you first come here. I didn't know anyone, I'd left all my family behind, I had never lived in the jungle before. I became a soldier at the Front for six years! But now I am a teacher.'

The Karen boast of the education they provide for children in rebel territory. There are schools in every forest village; any educated young man or woman is recruited as a teacher. But skilled manpower is in terribly short supply, so True Love also had to be a soldier, and an accountant. Indeed, the work they gave him knew no limits. A military ceremony to be organised, a French or American military advisor to be escorted, the Army budget to be sorted, the Health Department needing a new boat, a recording to be made of revolutionary Karen songs: True Love did it all. Sometimes the Education Department would obtain a video from Thailand, and

True Love would find a generator and television, set them up on the school steps and we could all watch old kung fu movies, huddled in blankets as the damp of the forest night closed in around us.

He was also my minder and escort in the Health Department. In return, I helped him build a house. He'd been married for a year but had no home, so he'd been given a month off his duties to do it. It was a simple structure on wooden stilts with a tin roof. We put in a bamboo floor and walls. The house became usable bit by bit, and True Love and his wife Silver moved in before it was finished.

One day, out together on the river, he told me what courtship was like for a Karen working for the rebel government.

'First you must inform the Head of your Department. Usually you must have worked for seven years before you marry: I was given special permission because I was getting old. So, then I proposed. I was very nervous. I took Silver on a river trip and we visited romantic places in the jungle – and she said yes.'

'Well, we don't get married in a church here, not even the Christians. We use a hall or the school. Any senior official can marry us, so I asked my Colonel from the Army. We wore traditional Karen dress, we had the school choir and some cakes and drinks. All very simple. The next day we went back to our work.'

But weddings could be far from simple for those who'd saved a bit of money: flower-decked bamboo arbours, gifts for all, a roast pork feast for two hundred, possibly beef also; the morning before one wedding I watched a cow being led behind a thicket to have its head whacked with the back of an axe and its throat cut promptly. I noticed that a number of young soldiers seemed to be involved.

'Who's in charge of the cooking?' I asked Pastor Moses.

'The defence militia. It's part of their training.'

This groom worked for the rebel Mines Department, and his Mines colleagues pitched in. In one corner of the kitchen, heaps of new banana leaves were stacked as platters for the chefs. In another corner, a pungent stack of meat, already moving with flies; in another, a heap of yams. The chefs laid about it all with eighteen-inch parangs. Mines Department wives clustered in the shade beneath the house making cane and cardboard baskets for the ceremony while children cut out little white paper flowers. In the late afternoon the soldiers lit fires in newly dug pits. By early evening, the stews were easily minded by one or two lads stirring with a wooden oar. Most people were lazing in hammocks, but then moved to the school where Mines had provided entertainment: a selection of Thai martial arts movies.

At nine in the morning, the groom appeared walking to the school with a small choir trailing him, singing hymns. He was wearing Karen traditional dress, sort of, the red striped smock over a crisp white shirt, white trousers and white shoes, his smock enhanced with a pink rose and a spray of ferns cut in the forest. The bride was in a long white Karen dress with delicate stripes of green, orange and red at the throat, pretty as can be. Her face, lightly powdered, was pale and silken.

And then Pastor Moses performed the ceremony just as at any Baptist church anywhere in the world. With a little homily; there's an old Karen song in which husbands and wives agree: if the wife sees crows flying overhead and says that they are cranes, her husband should agree, yes, those are cranes. But the people are exhorted to follow the example of the cranes and crows, which keep strictly to their own sort.

There was one nurse in the Karen Health Department who, I had to admit, I more than admired. Mature and clever, kind and very beautiful too – who would not? True Love and other friends teased me about it endlessly: why don't you marry her? But what would I be doing: either condemning myself to living in a non-state fighting an unwinnable war, or condemning her to pushing trolleys around Aberdeen supermarkets.

I put it well out mind, until one day I saw a wedding photograph pinned to a wall, the bride in Karen dress. The groom was a tall white man; I asked True Love, who could this selfless person be?

'He's a French mercenary,' said True Love.

5. ON THE RIVER

I had come downriver to buy a dug-out canoe. True Love knew the villages of the Karen rebels well, and thought this was the place: a grubby collection of huts on the riverbank. It was frequented by merchants with powerful six-wheel drive trucks who crossed into Burma illegally from Thailand along forest tracks, bringing everything from medicines to nylon shirts and prawn crackers. Here they met Karen traders who would carry these goods away on boats and along the forest paths deep into Burma itself, taking care to avoid the Burmese army. In the other direction, cattle smugglers took Burmese animals out to Thailand. The village had a cut-throat, frontier feel.

There was a small harbour, and a row of temporary bamboo shops on the muddy bluff above. When the rains began, the river would rise and sweep these away for another year. In the shops, the Karen sold forest specialities: anteaters, songbirds and wild honey, and giant edible monitor lizards tied up in their own tails and blinking resentfully. On benches outside, Karen sat munching banana fritters and listening for the motors of newly arrived boats.

So, this was the place to buy. We needed a sturdy new boat, which would last several years. It must be stable and large enough to carry four or five nurses from the rebel Government's Health Department. We ourselves would fit a platform at the back and a long-tail motor, the propeller trailing four feet behind.

After protracted negotiation, we found the perfect vessel; I paid for it in Thai currency, 1000 baht.

My problems had hardly begun. I spent long hours painting the new boat with black bitumen paint. Bartholomew, my Health Department boss, stood in it, rocked side to side and declared it unstabl – so I strapped two massive bamboo tubes to the sides as outriggers. We brought in a two-stroke engine from Thailand, but it was a fake, a copy of a European original, and was forever going wrong. I learned the first crucial lesson for Burmese river travel: abundant patience.

When the motor failed, we would sit on a sandbank while our boatman took it to pieces yet again, cursing when he dropped bits into the brown swirling river but contriving to make some spare part out of a rusty nail and bits cut from a tin can. Other boats passing would always stop to lend spanners and opinions on the repair.

The river is central to the life of the rebel Karen Free State, the key to communications, transport and defence. River travel changed dramatically, season by season. In the dry months, when the river was low we crept along painfully slowly, Bartholomew standing with a pole in the bow watching for the jagged rocks that could punch a hole in our hull. Sometimes the river flowed slow and tranquil, like a sheet of glass between the endless green of the thickly forested hills. When the river was full, rushing downstream was a thrill, with the rapids a tumult of white water but the rocks safely below us.

Coming up rapids with a full boat was often more than the motor could manage, however. We'd stop, unload everything and carry the baggage through the forest, while the boatman and his crew planned a line of attack. Then we'd hear the motor revved and cries of encouragement, and see them rushing at a gap, frantically steering, poling, pushing, shouting. Sometimes they'd be up in one go, yelling triumphantly. Sometimes the propeller would strike a rock and shatter, and the crew would hang on to a rock or branch while the boatman bolted on a new one mid-stream.

I delighted in our river trips, with True Love as the military escort, plus Bartholomew, myself and our young nurses. True Love would sit with his rifle scanning the river banks, supposedly watching out for Burmese patrols but in reality more interested in shooting monkeys or a wild chicken for dinner. We'd move through the forest watching the kingfishers zip back and forth, the monkeys in the trees, or the turtles popping their heads up alongside us. We listened to the bamboo cracking open in the heat with a noise like gunfire. We also listened for real gunfire. There were points on the river where the Burmese Army had pushed the Karen forces back, and had set up machine-gun posts. At these points, one got out and walked.

We would arrive at a remote village, go to the headman's house and install ourselves and our hammocks. We'd hand over the rice supply we carried, and soon we'd be feasted on rice and chicken curries. Then there'd be laughter, stories and cigars until we slept, waking in the chill forest morning to see villagers already gathering for our clinic, at which the girls learned to deal with everything from malaria to childbirth. Then after rice, fried fish and tea, we'd be on our way downriver.

On these Burmese rivers, there are not enough boats to go round. So, it is accepted that one give lifts. At the slightest hint of a journey, I would find a cluster of silent Karen waiting by the riverside with bags and boxes with no more intention of asking than a British commuter writes to ask permission of British Rail. But this was my boat, and I did like to be asked.

One morning, setting off on a long journey downstream with my trainee nurses, I found a young man sitting in the boat with a large tin box. I said I was sorry, we already had a full load. He didn't move. After a moment, I lifted out the box myself. The young man got out, picked up the box and returned it to the boat. I took it out, he put it back.

'True Love,' I asked, 'What's going on?'

But True Love wouldn't say. At last, the young man sadly took himself off.

'Come on, True Love,' I insisted, 'tell me.'

True Love looked slightly shifty, then explained.

'He was one of our soldiers. He was wounded in the head, and nearly died. He recovered, but began to act strangely. He knew he was ill, so he asked Colonel Marvel to release him from our army. He has been trying to get downriver for two weeks, just waiting for someone to give him a lift home.'

I felt dreadful, but it was too late. The young man had disappeared back into the forest.

6. BOARDERS

As head of the Karen rebel authorities Health Department, it was Bartholomew's job to organise the training of nurses to work in the villages of our territory. It was my job to teach them. So Bartholomew had my new bamboo house constructed next door to Boarders.

Boarders was the trainees' hostel, an unlovely barracks on high stilts with a tin roof that was home to twenty girls. Each staked a floor claim with a tin trunk, a woven plastic sleeping mat and a thin blanket. From the walls hung shirts and small mirrors. Boarders was bleak and noisy, and the girls often preferred to study or snooze in peace on my verandah, but at night, a glimmer of lamplight filtered out through the split bamboo walls, and I would hear the students singing or telling Karen stories, making it homely – though there were usually one or two girls shivering under blankets with malaria.

Some of them were orphans from the fighting, from districts captured and villages destroyed by the Burmese army; in Karen tradition, orphans are often associated with ill fortune. Some had seen their parents shot in front of their eyes. Some had been sent by their families or their villages to learn a useful skill, and were supposed to return in due course to be the local health worker. All of them were homesick. They did their best to keep each other cheerful. I brought them a volleyball from Thailand; they chopped a court out of the undergrowth and played with loud shrieks, while their friends sewed new pillows to stuff with raw kapok from the trees that grew around Boarders.

Bartholomew did his best to be avuncular. He provided Boarders with rice, plastic flip-flops and a roll of green plastic sheeting embossed with roses which he cut into rain capes for them. And he gave them, to look after, two small babies – orphans also of a sort. The father was a soldier in the Karen Army whose gun had accidentally killed his own wife. There were other relatives, but the babies had too much bad luck for anyone to want them. So they were given to Boarders, with twenty young mothers instead of one. The girls would take it in turns to look after the babies, and would spend the afternoon with them swinging in hammocks slung in the shade below the hostel.

Bartholomew was responsible for all the waifs and strays that forty years of war had washed up in our district. One of these was the Pu Payor, which means 'Burmese Grandad.'

For it was only the Burmese Army that was the enemy, never the Burmese people. The Pu Payor was a very elderly and decrepit Burmese mine worker. I never learned quite how he had arrived, but he had no family and was destitute. Bartholomew gave him a small plot of land among the banana trees near to my house and Boarders, where he built himself a tiny wooden hut. He was granted dining rights at the Boarders kitchen, and would collect a bowl of rice from there twice a day. He cultivated a little vegetable garden, and gathered the fruits of the forest. In spite of his age, he was as tough and supple as an old vine, being half my size but with twice my strength. He had false teeth and a disgusting old pipe, a frayed sarong and a straw bowler. He spent all his days fixing things, borrowing my tools to make shelves, lamps, doors and porches, and complex bamboo rainwater systems for both his hut and my house. He pottered, he tinkered: a new latch or ladder, an improved wooden dog dish. He stole a heavy free-standing Buddhist shrine from a Thai sawmill, carried it home in triumph and installed it just outside his hut, cutting a hole in the wall through which to gaze at it.

Bartholomew gave the Pu Payor certain duties. When we acquired a small flock of goats, the Pu Payor was made Master of the Goats. Unfortunately, he understood none of their appetites. Soon they demolished gardens and reduced the one wretched nanny to a pale shadow of a goat, vastly pregnant. In recompense, he made her a lean-to shelter with a fire for the winter.

He was also appointed Head Gardener of the Health Department. He built stout bamboo fences in a vain attempt to keep the goats off the vegetable gardens, the lime and jackfruit trees, and wheezed thin oaths at the Boarders girls when they picked fruit without permission. They regarded him as a grubby old man, and teased him mercilessly. One day, howls of rage came from the Pu Payor's hut: the girls had found the trunk of a rotten banana palm, and had rolled it up in his bedding.

The Pu Payor kept me well supplied with bananas and limes, and tended the little flowerbeds about both our houses. He would collect jackfruit seeds for me, and boil them up in dark red water in a greasy black tin over the goat's winter fire. In return, I would walk across in the evening with mugs of sweet coffee and a gift of tinned sardines. We had no words in common but we did fine, pointing at the pregnant nanny goat, the stars, his flowers or the shrine and grunting at each other in peaceable satisfaction.

He was a dead shot with a catapult. Sometimes, the little old man would accompany us on boat trips with the trainee nurses, and I would have to stop him slaughtering every fish-eagle on the river.

But the river finally got the better of him. Some months after I left Burma, I received a letter from True Love with all the gossip.

Amongst other news, he wrote that the Pu Payor had been found dead in the river one morning, his corpse stiff and cold. Bartholomew's elder son had dragged him out, but the Boarders girls wouldn't touch him; they had too much bad luck to cope with already.

7. COME QUICK

When a shooting star passes overhead, the Karen people of Burma say that a boy in the Heavens is going to visit his girlfriend. But the Karen have always had a reputation for stern morals. The rebels of the Karen Free State tried hard to uphold this reputation: it marked them out as different from the wicked Burmese. But it gave them headaches. Come Quick was a nurse, one of my students. By sending her to the bamboo jail for premarital sex, the rebel authorities reduced our nursing staff by 10%. It was a severe blow. Bartholomew, my boss and the head of the local Health Department, was near despair.

Come Quick got her name because her own birth had been very quick and easy. Some people thought Come Quick a shameless hussy. She was young and attractive in a tomboyish way, but had a gap in her front teeth which we often teased her about. She was also a prize flirt. With True Love as my military escort, I took her on tour through rebel territory, up and down the river in our dugout canoe, holding impromptu clinics in the forest villages. True Love, in uniform and carrying a carbine, looked very manly. Come Quick just looked a baggage. In one village there was a young teacher called Milly. True Love said that I was in love with Milly, and declared that Come Quick was crazy with jealousy. I grinned at her – and she came after me with a machete, chasing me round the compound and actually succeeding in cutting my finger – after which she went to find medicinal leaves in the forest, rubbed them to a pulp with her spittle and used this to dress my wound.

When her training was finished, Bartholomew sent her south to work at a Karen refugee camp. But a week later, she was back. She was pregnant.

The village lads were merciless:

'We demanded to know, where? How many times? We got it out of her. Six times, out in the forest! She'd told the other nurses she was going to gather vegetables.'

Before I learned who the father was, Come Quick was in jail, sentenced to three months for fornication. Come Quick's lover was a rebel soldier who was sent back to the Front Line in disgrace. But Bartholomew's problems with his nurses were not over yet.

Rosepetal, another nurse, caused further embarrassment. She had gone south to the same refugee camp as Come Quick. Within a month, she too was back. Her lover was a young soldier called David, who manned a border post where the Karen levied a toll on Burma-Thai smuggling. David had in fact asked the Finance Office for permission to marry Come Quick, and the Finance Office had asked Bartholomew as Head of the Health Department. But Bartholomew had refused. He was desperately short staffed, had supported Rosepetal throughout her schooling, and now needed her services.

Now, here she was back at Headquarters. 'Rosepetal has to get married,' said True Love, 'for the same reason Come Quick had to get married. We can't send Rosepetal to jail; she's too valuable.'

The wedding was a grim affair. Everyone knew that Rosepetal and David were in disgrace. The presiding officials were in a foul mood and wouldn't stay to tea. The choir of other nurses were jealous, and sang badly. And there should have been a pork banquet for the whole village, but the soldier detailed to shoot the pig bungled the job. He missed the pig's heart and it ran off into the forest.

So the young couple were rehabilitated, after a fashion. My boatman, who considered himself a traditionalist, was unimpressed. In his view, the Karen rebellion was undermining traditional village morals.

'Why are all these girls pregnant in the first place?' he demanded. 'Is that what good Karen maidens should be thinking of? In my home village, if a father catches his daughter speaking to a strange man he is very angry and sends her to the kitchen at once. We should have patrols at nightfall, and less grass and bananas.'

'Less grass and bananas?' I was bewildered. 'What do you mean?'

'There are too many places to hide,' he declared. 'They like to go out and… well, sort of, get married among the bananas.'

I saw Come Quick in jail, sitting in a bamboo hut with four other women, all there for offences against morality. I asked someone, who exactly had sent her there?

They said, 'This is a special law made by our general. He is a very strict man, and believes that our revolution will not prosper if we behave improperly. The penalty is one to three months – unless the man is a Front Line soldier; we would need him too badly.'

Other men went to jail. Of the work party who built my timber and bamboo house near the hospital, several were adulterers. There were twenty men in the lock-up at the time. Three were murderers, the other seventeen all guilty of illegitimate love.

'What's more,' said my stern boatman, 'three of them are Baptist pastors from the villages!'

In traditional Karen society, the punishments for adultery were much worse. In the 1920s, the death penalty still applied. The guilty pair were brought before the village headman. On a table were placed three identical pills, one harmless, the other two containing a deadly poison. The man and woman were required to chose and swallow one each. They then walked out into the forest together. After one hour, the villages elders followed them to find either both dead, or one still alive. In the latter case, the survivor was allowed home to lead a normal life.

Usually the rebel Free State was more merciful, but when a woman at Headquarters abandoned her husband and took not one but two new lovers, the General got to hear of it and had all three shot.

Bartholomew went off to the jail one morning and returned with Come Quick. All was forgiven amidst welcoming laughter, and soon her baby was born. Come Quick was immensely proud. Meanwhile, my boatman told me to give up any thoughts of Milly in the village downriver. He was sure her father wouldn't let her love a white man.

'Did we ever meet Milly's father?' I asked True Love. 'I don't remember him.'

'He wasn't there,' said True Love. 'He's one of the pastors now in jail for adultery.'

8. GREAT LAKE

The Karen of Burma are, at heart, forest and river people. The villages of the rebel Karen National Union are almost all sited by rivers. To tour the villages, I needed a boat and a skilled boatman who could handle the rapids. I had one of the best; his name was Great Lake.

Great Lake was a charming 33-year old who, when piloting our dug-out canoe down rapids with an expression of exhilarated concentration on his handsome face, could look very like Errol Flynn playing Captain Blood. The boat had a motor with a long prop shaft that trailed four feet behind. To steer, Great Lake sat on a tiny wooden platform, wearing a sarong, a green beret and generally with a fat Burmese cheroot in his mouth.

He was not, however, a regular employee of the rebel Health Department, not a 'member of the Revolution' at all. He said he was too lazy. He helped out because he loved to travel.

Great Lake was a huntsman and trader. He lived in a wooden house that he'd built on the river bank near mine with his wife Lili and his small babies. The house was also the shop, with cupboards on the verandah stuffed with cigars and torch batteries, shampoo, biscuits and a few clothes also. I would often join them for Sunday breakfast. Being a good Baptist, Great Lake had written *No shopping Sunday* on the cupboard door. Having finished our monkey curry, I would take two cigars from the cupboard without permission to save him embarrassment, silently place money in the tin, then give him one. We'd lie back and smoke them peacefully, while his babies crawled over the bamboo slats of the floor urinating on the chickens below.

'No work today,' he'd say, 'only lazy.'

Great Lake, however, was discontented. Like so many civilians, he'd been pushed into the war against his will, because the Burmese had arrested his father and overrun his home village. Great Lake had drifted into rebel territory, trying his hand at cattle trading and tin mining before agreeing to be a mechanic for the rebel authorities.

But he didn't trust the leaders of the rebellion. He thought them incompetent, and he thought the whole business undermined Karen culture. Real Karen, he said, could make their own clothes, shoulder bags and fish paste for cooking. The rebels had forgotten how, and came to him to buy them.

'All they can make here is babies,' he scoffed. 'And look at them: the women cut their hair! No real Karen cuts her hair. They eat mishmash food which is nothing and they wear nylon shirts under their Karen tunics.'

He always refused to accept food or a permanent job, declaring himself independent. The trouble was, he wasn't a very competent trader. To begin with, he was absurdly generous, giving credit all round. Then, he gave his own family most of the biscuits.

'Your children are eating your profits,' I told him, but he smiled and said, 'I love my babies.'

And trade was too much like hard work. Once a week, Great Lake's wife traveled to the border to buy stock. But, with half the village trying to scrape a living from trade, the possible profits on a packet of biscuits were infinitesimal. There were endless risks. They bought a batch of boat propellers – but they were the wrong size; nobody wanted them. They bought powdered coffee – but it turned out to be *Coffee Mate* whitener, equally useless. On the difficult haul in, over forest tracks, things got broken and squashed.

They even tried buying a huge block of ice and smuggling it in over the Thai border. They buried it by a well-used path near the hospital packed in sawdust together with a crate of fizzy drink, and Great Lake's sister swung expectantly in a hammock nearby, but there were few passing locals with enough spare cash for cold drinks, and the ice melted first.

Sometimes Great Lake would find exotic items in the forest and trade them with Thais. One of these was the gall-bladder of a mountain bear, a rarity much valued as medicine by the Bangkok Chinese. Great Lake was enormously excited, and presented it to a Thai he thought trustworthy – but somehow he never saw the money.

Still, he kept trying. One morning he called to me excitedly:

'I caught a deer in the river! It was swimming, it's a baby, like a dog, swimming across and I was swimming too and I caught in my hands! I've sold it to the Thais.'

There was also a little white monkey that lived for a time on his verandah, and a baby anteater. They were all sold to Thailand. Venison went the same way. Lazy or not, Great Lake was a good hunter.

'I know where to find deer. At this time of year they are calling to their lady friends so we pick some grass and put it in our mouths and make a kissing noise, so they come very close to be kissed and we shoot them.'

Great Lake was the best possible company on river trips, both because he was skilful, and because he took my safety and education seriously. He declared that I should have a traditional Karen torch-cosy. Every Karen carries their flashlight in a knitted woollen sheath. Being 'lazy', Great Lake didn't actually make this himself; he got his sister to do it, with the words *Peace and Love* in the design. Great Lake just made the long shoulder strap.

He would sometimes help with the medical work. I wanted to do a village population survey. I explained the system, and we divided the houses between us. When I set off, with the headman to guide me, Great Lake remained lounging on the verandah, sucking a cigar.

'What are you waiting for?' I called.

'I am waiting till you are out of sight. Then I'm going to make up the answers here,' he replied. 'I am *too* lazy!'

But he could not always prevent the sadness surfacing through his gaiety. He would sit on my porch at night, listening to the BBC Burmese service reports of the war. It made him restless.

'I cannot stand this. I want to go back to my home. My father is all alone now; I want to plant a farm and help him.'

'But you told me you're lazy and hate farming,' I said.

'Well, yes,' he said. 'I'd better employ Burmese to do it for me.'

9. RED STAR

Throughout the history of South Asia, the elephant has been a symbol of power and majesty. Elephants have been used in war, to carry Rajahs and to trample criminals to death. More recently, elephants were the means by which great teak trees were felled and dragged to the rivers to be floated to sawmills downstream. The Karen people of Burma are the most skilful elephant trappers, trainers and handlers. Thus, when the Karen began their rebellion against the Burmese government in 1949, it was not long before there were elephants with the rebel forces.

The rebel Karen army use the elephants for jungle patrols, and for carrying supplies and ammunition. When I first came to Karen territory, elephants carried my bags. There were problems; elephants are quite thin skinned, and this creature met a swarm of bees which drove it, maddened, into the forest till it smacked its head on a tree. One baby elephant uprooted my neighbour's fruit garden. Another put its trunk through the clinic window and started playing with the microscopes. But the animals were enormously valuable; when one was killed by a falling tree, the village family was ruined. And they were wonderful to ride. In thick jungle one day, my elephant driver turned our animal onto a steep muddy slope. To my delight, the elephant tobogganed down the mud on its belly.

Red Star was a freelance elephant trapper contracting to the Karen army. He was in his thirties, the gentlest of people, a man who seemed to desire nothing more than a life of peace and seclusion in the forest. He had no family, only his elephants.

I was introduced by Great Lake, my boatman and Red Star's closest friend. Red Star had come looking for help. He had a she-elephant which had recently given birth, and the baby's umbilical stump had become infected. We took sprays and antiseptics and went upriver in a tiny fishing canoe, no more than a scraped out log in which we poled gently upstream.

Red Star had brought the elephant here to give birth in tranquillity, away from the village. At a bend in the river, he and his assistants had built a shelter in the forest, a wobbly structure of bamboo just big enough for two blanket rolls and the usual Karen clutter: a shoulder bag, a gun, and a toothbrush tucked into the frame. In front of the hut a fire smouldered and suspended over it were two dark and shrivelled objects. One was the elephant's umbilicus, the other was the stomach of a porcupine. Both were being smoked, for sale to apothecaries in Thailand.

Twenty yards away, the elephant was chained to a tree. Her baby, a week old, never left its mother's side – nor would it until its army training began at the age of seven. Its eyes were bright and pink-rimmed while its mother's were tired and grey. The baby's trunk was an encumbrance that it hadn't mastered, and which flopped about like a massive worm pinned to its face, getting in the way when it tried to feed. The mother shifted uneasily at my presence, throwing an arc of dirt and leaf-mould. But she showed no concern when Red Star knelt by her baby's side and sprayed the wound.

One hundred years ago, wild elephants were numerous in these forests. Now Red Star had trouble finding them. He would often join us in the Health Department boat, travelling throughout rebel territory for news.

'How does he trap them?' I asked Great Lake.

'A camouflaged pit. The elephant falls in, they put ropes around it and light fires to stop the animal sleeping for three days. Then it will not fight you. But you must teach it elephant-Burmese so that it knows what you want it to do.'

'Elephants speak Burmese?' I asked.

'Well,' he said, 'if you want it to work on the Thai border, it must know Thai also.'

One day, sitting with Red Star on Great Lake's verandah, I found a cheap plastic pipe, picked it up and played a tune. Great Lake was unimpressed; clearly I needed real Karen music.

'I wish I could find it,' I said. 'I asked True Love, but he can only play Country and Western.'

'Red Star can do it!' said Great Lake.

I couldn't believe my luck. A deal was quickly struck: I would bring them a radio from Thailand. In return, Red Star would make me not just a Karen jew's harp but a lyre as well. I just had to provide guitar strings for it.

Some weeks later, I went to collect. The rains had begun and Red Star had moved to a larger forest hut with the rest of his team. There were five of them in all. In the new house of springy bamboo, sunlight streamed in through the slatted walls from all sides, making patterns of hatching and herringbone over everything within.

All five elephant trappers were involved in making the instruments. The wood had been pre-prepared, dried and hardened over the fire. Now the lyre was made, a single section of giant bamboo for the soundbox, covered with a soundboard made from an old biscuit tin beaten to shape, and fitted with a long curved neck and six strings. It sounded lovely. Then they made three jew's harps, cutting them from hardened cane. Each was made at speed but with infinite care, the tongues shaved minutely for a clean note, the finished items rubbed with beeswax and toasted over the fire. The elephant men were rather surprised when I could play the jew's harp as well as the rest of them – but even Great Lake didn't know the songs that Red Star sang as he played the lyre.

'These,' said Great Lake, 'are very old and difficult songs.'

But most beautiful of all was a Karen hunting horn. Red Star made it from the beak of a hornbill, eight inches long with a glowing orange tip. It had a hole cut in the side and a metal reed cut from an old cartridge case, held in place with beeswax. It made a thin but piercing note. Red Star gave it to me.

'There,' said Great Lake, 'now you may go safely anywhere in the forest. If the Burmese hear this they will cry that the Karen are attacking – and they will run for their lives!'

10. BISMARCK

When I first arrived in rebel Karen territory, entering Burma illegally on muddy forest tracks over the border from Thailand into the Karen Free State, it was raining hard. That first night, I was given lodging on the verandah of a dark and dusty house where I first experienced a bed of solid teak (with no mattress). I was exhausted, and noticed little except the ants that invaded my mosquito net in the early hours. The rain crashed down through the forest to roar upon the tin roof. In the morning I found that I was sharing with a family of five refugees, fleeing from Burma.

Over the months I met scores of refugees. Most were Karen, their villages burned and their families murdered. But others were simple Burmese, for whom the eccentric cruelties of that country had become unbearable. It has never been easy to leave Burma. Before the British came, under the old Kings, any attempt to depart might be regarded as treason. Men were rarely granted permission; women, never. Today, thousands have fled up into rebel areas or across the frontier into Thailand, but they have no status, no papers, no passports. They are stuck.

This young couple were of very mixed blood. Bismarck's father was a German who had come to Rangoon after the Second World War, bought a cinema and made his own Burmese films, love stories mostly. He'd fitted out a lorry as a mobile cinema, toured the Delta and married a local girl. Bismarck's wife was called Judith, and her father was a French businessman who had fallen in love with a Karen girl, married her and then killed himself with drink and tobacco.

Judith was a young teacher when she met and married Bismarck, a student at Rangoon University. He was a political activist and, by the time their first daughter was born, he was already under police surveillance. In 1974 he was caught up in riots in Rangoon, and arrested.

'They gave me one helluva beating and torture,' he told me. 'They sat me on a block of ice and gave me electrical shocks. They dripped water on my head, drip drip drip. It's quite nice at first but after one and a half hours the sound is like little hammers breaking open the skull and I was ready to scream.'

By the time he'd been arrested and tortured a second and a third time, his health was broken. They now had children. Judith was badly frightened and could not support them all. She told Bismarck that they must leave Burma. They would have to escape across the border, which meant putting themselves in the hands of the rebel Karen. Judith's memory of the journey was clearer than Bismarck's:

'We travelled down the coast by bus, then upriver to a small village in the hills. Then we began to walk. We were escorted by Karen soldiers and there were others going with us to the Karen Free State. Bismarck was really sick now. At times his malaria was really bad, he was almost unconscious and we had to carry him. We had three babies with us too! I carried the little one, the other two walked the whole way, they did not complain. There were snakes and monkeys, I was really scared.'

I said that I thought the Karen were more dangerous to the monkeys than vice versa, but Judith wasn't having it.

'How could we know? We'd never done anything like this; we're from Rangoon! I thought the monkeys would steal our babies.

Bismarck was worse, he was really very funny. If he saw a wild buffalo, he'd run and hide!'

They reached Headquarters and Bismarck was asked to teach in a new school there. But at once his health broke down and Judith had to nurse him.

Within moments of meeting Bismarck you could see that the whole story was true. He was a slight and delicate figure in a red sarong, nervous and excitable. He was unable to sit still but could do nothing of much use. Indeed, his arm was badly scalded from a misguided attempt to intervene in the kitchen. He was now just another child for the calm, endlessly patient Judith to nurse. Moreover, in the malarial damp of the forest, the health and morale of the children was deteriorating.

'When I am recovered,' said Bismarck, 'I will teach here. I must repay these people somehow. Judith has a sister in the United States. If that woman can send us a lot of money, we can buy Thai passports and go to the US. That is the only thing for us now.'

'What does Judith's sister do?' I asked.

'She's a waitress,' he said.

Four months later, I met them again at a refugee camp in the south. They'd been given a cramped and squalid hut – just a shelter with a dirt floor and a bamboo sleeping platform at the back. The children, meek and sweet, were being as little trouble as possible, but the youngest was sick and flushed. I produced some aspirin. Judith, between giving the child drinks and wrapping her tighter in blankets, sat on the ground in the open shelling castor oil nuts for which work she could earn a few pennies. Bismarck, as nervous and twitchy as ever, hung about chattering.

'There are many cobras in the long grass here. Also there are wild cats which are taking my chickens. Also we are sent here to work, you see they have a new school now and they need me. I am almost well although I am hellish tired sometimes. Judith is almost well…'

We didn't dwell on it, but talked of America instead.

I have a photograph of Judith and Bismarck on the steps of the rest-house, my first day in the Karen Free State. The young man is pale and thin, his expression anxious. Judith stands just behind him. As she sat later in her bamboo hut waiting for money from the waitress in America, she must sometimes have thought back to her life in the dilapidated but beautiful city of Rangoon with its golden pagodas, where she had her family and her job, her house and her relatives – above all her eldest child whom she will probably never see again. And she must, sometimes, have wondered what possessed her to marry a young man with dangerous political notions. But Burma is full of such quietly courageous people. In my photograph, Judith looks careworn but calm, strong and very patient.

11. RICE

When the Karen people of Burma look up the stars and see the Milky Way, they call it the Rice Bin. No people in the world love rice quite like the rebels of the Karen Free State. When we in Britain meet an acquaintance, we enquire after their health, but the Karen ask, 'Have you finished your rice?'

They consumed fantastic quantities of it. One of our Health team regularly ate five heaped platefuls at a sitting – and then complained of indigestion. In any forest house there is a battered pot of cold rice from which you can help yourself to a snack. On tour, with my paramedic colleagues in the forest, they would carry cold cooked rice in plastic bags and eat it along the way.

All this left the rebel authorities with a problem. The rebel state near the Thai border occupies forested hills. The hill Karen grow some rice, but not enough to feed the Karen National Liberation Army, let alone all the functionaries like True Love, Bartholomew and myself.

So the Karen authorities must purchase rice from Thailand and distribute it to their people, while encouraging their villagers to grow more. But that in its turn is dangerous, for the Burmese Army knows very well that the villagers feed the rebels. If they are caught concealing stocks of rice, the Burmese punish them brutally. There is an old adage which Karen mothers use with their children: *Eat quickly, the Burmese are coming.*

From time to time, we would all have to collect our rice from the frontier. One day, I saw the entire population of our village set off walking up the muddy hill to the border fifteen kilometres away, and

100

in the afternoon they returned exhausted, adults and tiny children all with bags of rice on their heads. It was cheap stuff, the grain broken and cracked.

'Do you know what they do with this muck in Thailand?' said True Love. 'They feed it to the pigs.'

At Bartholomew's house we ate twice a day, crouched on the floor round a low circular table. Each person had an enamel plate heaped with rice in front of them. As the family gathered, each person touched the rice, breaking it up with their fingers, making contact with it but not eating till Bartholomew had said grace. Then we'd mix the rice with a little fish paste, drink from the communal bowl of soup and start on the serious business of stuffing in as much rice as we could.

We ate well. Traditional forest Karen eat little but rice and fish, but Bartholomew's family would contrive curries of pawpaws and lizard eggs, fried banana flowers, dried shredded venison and baby mangoes, noodles and nuts. On Sunday mornings Moses the pastor would often invite me to breakfast which he cooked himself; there I was introduced to stews of mountain bear and wild cat. On tour with True Love and the team, we ate curried otter and green pigeons.

In one of their old commandments, the Karen ancestors declared: *O Children and grandchildren, we may eat anything without sin, for God created them all for us.* The Karen, indeed, eat almost anything except dog – although there is a tribe in Thailand who eat dogs regularly. They were enthusiastic hunters, always on the watch for something good. One day, when I was walking with True Love and a military escort through the forest, the boys shot a large monkey and asked permission to stop and eat it. It was a wonderful display of forest skills. Almost without discussion, the soldiers divided up the tasks. One made a fire and boiled water. Another produced a handful of onions and a small plastic bag of spices, and made a sauce. A third cut thick bamboos and cunningly fashioned mugs and dishes. The meat was stewed, the monkey's head tossed onto the fire to roast. The hands and feet, held in split lengths of bamboo, were propped up around the fire to grill. The triumphant marksman got the brains, while his pals got the hands to nibble.

I got used to the diet eventually, and came to enjoy most of it. There was one item, however, that I never developed a taste for. It was a condiment for rice, a dark brown sauce. It was made from fermented monkey faeces. The monkey is a herbivore, so its gut is full of greenery. This would be squeezed out into a bamboo tube, sealed and hung up in the sun to ferment, then mixed with salt. It had a curiously acrid savour.

The food that held greatest significance for the rebel Free State apart from rice was pork. At any wedding, a pig would be slaughtered. But, just as importantly, communal pig feasts would be held for each village in rebel territory on any special occasion. So, for the Karen New Year, or for Karen Revolution Day, or the end of the school year, long tables of bamboo would be built in the shade of the kapok trees, with benches for everyone. In the past, these feasts had often symbolised the expiation of sin from the village; now they signified the unity of the people, their solidarity in face of the Burmese enemy. They were splendid, joyful occasions.

Huge cauldrons of rice would be boiled, and the tables covered with plates of rice, boiled plantain and dishes of pork, fat and bristle included. There'd be a first sitting of senior men and army officers, with the schoolgirls rushing around serving, carrying the rice to the tables in huge steaming baskets. Then everyone joined in the feast, soldiers and children, old grannies and visiting traders, and restraint and order collapsed into cheerful gluttony while the dogs scrapped for the pork fat.

At one such feast, the schoolchildren cooked for their teachers. The Education Department had scrounged a little money, and every child received a plastic bag with six new exercise books, three ballpoint pens, a box of coloured crayons and a Bible Story colouring book, together with a handful of sweets and custard creams. I stood by a young soldier smiling with delight as he surveyed his comrades and village friends gorging themselves.

'What are you so happy about?' I asked.

He replied, he was thinking of the Burmese generals who were trying to strangle the life out of the rebellion by cutting off the food supply. Looking again at the laughing children, he said,

'If those generals could see us now, they would cry! They would cry!'

12. BAT SHIT GUNS

The Karen people began their present war of Independence against the government of Burma more than forty years ago. But they have been fighting the Burmese, off and on, for centuries. They were always a minority, and they are often described as gentle people: one journalist called them 'the world's most pleasant and civilised guerrilla group.'

They had, nonetheless, a reputation for cunning and for certain skills that were invaluable in a guerrilla war. Amongst these was the manufacture of firearms.

Guns have been popular in Burma and Thailand since perhaps the 14th Century. In almost any Karen forest home there is a gun, which might well be home-made.

In the village where I was training young nurses, I watched my friend and boatman Great Lake making a musket for Red Star the elephant trainer. A local shop sold him a length of steel tube for the barrel. Great Lake made everything else, the wooden stock, the spring trigger and percussion cap mechanism. It was beautifully done, and complete with sights and a ramrod tipped with a brass cartridge case.

I asked him, 'What do you use for gunpowder?'

He said, 'Bat shit.'

This is an ancient skill. The soil from the floor of caves where bats sleep is rich in nitrates from the droppings. You boil it up with ash, mixing the residue with sulphur and charcoal made from mango wood, and you have gunpowder.

'What about ammunition?' I asked Great Lake.

'Anything that fits,' he said. 'I have a friend who makes bullets by melting down broken boat propellers and pouring the metal into old torch bulbs.'

They used these guns for hunting. They made a glorious bang which sent all the forest wildlife into hiding for hours. There were dangers. I saw men and boys with their eyebrows gone and the skin tattooed by bursting muskets.

'I have another friend,' said Great Lake, 'who specialises in making mortars for our Karen Army. The ignition is an electric spark from a battery. He used it in a battle once against the Burmese, and fired three shots. They all went in completely different directions which was good because the Burmese were too confused to fire back. Then he showed it to our General. The first shot went very far, over the fields. The second went not so far, because it was all full of dirt. The third only went fifty yards and exploded. The general did not want his mortar. But we make other things that work very well. We once raided a Burmese airfield and shot down a helicopter with a home-made rocket launcher.'

But all their ingenuity cannot free the Karen from the dangers of guns in the home. One man came home from a hunting trip and placed his rifle on the table. His 2 year-old daughter reached up and touched the trigger. The shot hit the girl's mother in the stomach, killing her.

Meanwhile, both sides in this war use landmines. Soldiers have long known that smaller mines make bigger problems for the enemy. A dead person requires only burial, but a wounded or crippled person needs medical care, drugs and surgery, transport, nurses, and maybe years of welfare support. I saw, very often, the characteristic landmine victims, hit in the legs and the face. One former soldier, blinded in both eyes, with a damaged left hand and a stiff leg, made some sort of living by portering. He would collect goods from the Thai traders up at the border and stagger down the forest track to the riverside villages, feeling his way with a stick. Other victims were women and small children. Many of the mines are made in Britain, but the Karen characteristically retaliate with something home-made: they dig a pit in the forest path and conceal there a contraption made of razor-sharp bamboo blades. When the Burmese soldier tumbles in, the effect is most unpleasant.

The Karen are famous for more peaceable arts, however. They are some of the finest weavers in Asia. Traditionally this is done on a simple back-strap loom, and in the forest villages, women sit on their porches weaving the traditional tunics of thick red cloth with thin red stripes for the men, or long white gowns with thin red stripes for maidens, each finished off with a charming fringe. Few of the Revolutionaries wear these clothes daily, but on any national day or church celebration, traditional dress is *de rigueur*. To go with the tunics, men wear a dark red sarong – and to provide the cloth for this, the rebel authorities have established a special weaving mill.

Another famous skill is – or was – the casting of bronze drums. The drums are exceedingly ancient; instruments still exist which were made more than two thousand years ago. How the simple forest-dwelling Karen learned to cast these magnificent instruments is a great mystery. The drums are big and heavy, three feet deep and almost as broad. The bronze face is decorated with concentric rings and elaborate star patterns. On the edges are tiny figures of frogs and elephants which are now understood to represent the little Karen nation and their heavyweight persecutors the Burmese. The drums are the symbol of Karen independence, and the rebel soldiers wear a little badge of two hunting horns and a drum. I have one of these badges stuck to my computer in Edinburgh.

We had a bronze drum at the village where I lived and worked. Mostly it hung in the school. But on Revolution Day it was hung out on the football pitch with a guard of honour. True Love would rig up a PA system with a little generator, and Colonel Marvel would make speeches exhorting the village to try harder and to dig better air raid shelters. Then the huge and heavy drum would be carried back to safety in the school.

Once upon a time, every Karen village had a drum. The deep booming note of the drums calmed the forest spirits. A 19th century British officer described how the drums were played at festivals, and how, 'A scene of the wildest revelry ensues, the music softens the heart and women weep for friends they have lost.'

Today the drums are increasingly rare. Many were sold to dealers and to the kings of Thailand; now, any Karen who tries to export a drum is executed. The Karen have lost the skill of making them, and I'm afraid that is our fault. When the British took over Burma in the 19th century, the drums were still made in just one centre in the north. But the locals were refusing to pay any taxes, and the British sent a punitive expedition. The Karen drum-makers heard gunfire, abandoned the village and, carrying their drums, fled to the south. They never recommenced manufacture.

14. UNDERFOOT

In the Tenasserim forest I could have done with street lighting. This was not because I feared muggers or cars (there were neither), but because I was frightened of what was underfoot.

Around our riverside village the soil was a fine clay. In the dry season, it turned to a delicate fawn-coloured dust that swirled in little clouds and twisters as I walked – but the moment the rains struck, it became a greasy, cloying mud. Things lived in this mud. If only the things had stayed underground.

There were giant centipedes, eight or nine inches long and glossy dark brown. They had crimson jaws, their bite worse than any scorpion. They would come from their burrows and climb into village homes and into the family bedding, and lie snug along a child's flank – until the child turned over. It was claimed that small children sometimes died of the shock and pain.

I slept in a hammock, but sometimes needed to find my way in the dark to the bathroom, a patch of cement flooring with a rotting timber surround. The centipedes from the forest could enter beneath the ragged bottom edge of the boards but would not be able to find a way out, so my torch might pick out two or three creatures the size of small snakes scuffling around the damp cement perimeter, feeling for an exit.

I might be out of an evening without a torch. In Karen homes one always takes off one's shoes, and so habitually one wears light, easily removed sandals – in my case, rubber flip-flops. These were convenient, but provided no protection against centipedes. I would have to make my way home perhaps half a mile over soft, unlit mud.

I would skip hurriedly, feeling a shiver of disgust up my spine, filled with dread. Peering around the village, I would glimpse in silhouette my Karen friends skipping likewise.

At the outset of the rainy season, other beings awoke underground. On a dank afternoon sitting on someone's porch and peering out at the rain, I might see a crack in the mud, a patch of soil a few inches across heaving up and splitting, until out came a plume of termites. They had hatched all together, and would twizzle up from the earth in a slow gyrating cloud, flapping their ungainly translucent wings until they disappeared into the foliage overhead.

In the old days, one would have been watching for the tracks of tigers. When a passenger aircraft crashed into the forest not far away, our local commander, Colonel Marvel, informed the world's press that his men were searching for survivors but held out little hope as they had seen many tiger tracks in the mud. I doubt there had been a single tiger in the Tenasserim forests for many decades, but a political point was being made: 'Only we are at home in this place. It is ours.'

On my walking tours from village to village to train paramedics, I kept my eyes on the ground. The narrow path wound along the contours of thickly forested hills, and one could not see much: vegetation to left and right, the next turn in the path a few yards ahead. During World War Two it was reported of bored British troops marching in the jungle that they did not know what to think – literally. Some would recite passages from the Bible over and over. I wore a cotton sun hat to keep insects and foliage out of my hair, but this acted as an acoustic reflector and my thoughts would be numbed by the sound of the steady slap-slap of my feet on the mud.

Leeches were a particular grief. British soldiers wore anti-leech boots of heavy green canvas, with brass vents at the instep whose holes were too small for a leech to enter. But the water entered – there was plenty of water – and in no time one's feet became white, wrinkled and foul, prior to the development of trench foot. Conventional walking shoes were useless: they gave no protection, and merely filled with thin mud. So I and the boys of my escort wore sandals of various sorts; theirs were plastic beach shoes; mine were leather, and in water and mud they became impossibly slippery and slithered from side to side of my foot. But I dared not take them off.

Whatever we wore, we were caught by the leeches. There was one especially muddy path in the forest which ran beside a meandering stream; if one of my escort lost his footwear it would float gently away, and he would scamper to the next bend to intercept it. Along the path leeches waited, dangling from low fronds or standing upright on the mud and waving slightly as they sensed our approach. Within minutes, we would all have leeches fastened to us, sucking our blood. They would be on our calves, our ankles, or swelling luxuriantly between our toes.

After an hour's hurried walk, this path came to a sharp rise and here the leeches ended. We would light a small fire, and scorch them off our legs with smouldering twigs. My companion said:

'We have a medicine to make them fall off.'

'So everyone has been telling me: salt, tobacco and lime on a rag tied round a stick. Does it work?'

'It works!'

'So why does no one ever carry any?'

110

No answer.

Another friend told me cheerily:

'You know, we have special leeches that like buffaloes very much, and when a buffalo comes they climb up its back leg, go in its bottom and suck and suck until it dies.'

Nearby, the path wallowed in a pool of soft grey clay mud that was two foot deep, sloppy and clinging. There was little choice: one took off one's shoes and floundered forwards, trying not to grab at the trees that were covered in sharp spines, and trying also not to think about the neat round holes that punctuated the mud: snakes, or rats? Or possibly the land-crabs, coloured soft grey and magenta.

I saw very few snakes on the ground, perhaps only half a dozen adults, but in baby snake season I could come upon two or three together, new from the nest like fragments of string. They might one day be lethal, but not yet. I'd be confronted by a micro-viper snapping dramatically at me with a bite range of four inches. Thank goodness, their parents generally made themselves scarce when they heard (or felt) my sandals slapping on the ground.

Most scorpions were too small to cause trouble to the shod foot, but I moved with care nonetheless. I once met a giant scorpion, jet black and perhaps eight inches long like a jungle lobster. It sat in the middle of the path as though defying me to pass by, ready to lunge for my flesh. I was about to prod it when I had an appalling vision of the scorpion swarming up my stick towards my hand. I scurried past it and away.

The dangers on the ground might be man-made. The object for both sides in the war was not to kill – a dead enemy requires only burial – but to maim, so that the victim becomes a continuing focus of fear, and a burden of care. The rebels made caltrops of razor sharp bamboo which could be concealed in small hollows on the approaches to a village and which would shred an attacker's leg with wounds that would be slow to heal. The Burmese army used small land-mines to blow off feet and strip calf-muscles from the bone.

Forest paths quickly became overgrown. New stems soon sprouted, and had to be chopped away. But the sharpest machete cannot cut perfectly flush to the ground, and there were always stumps and jagged things to catch one's foot in the very centre of the trail. On the flat – walking along a forested ridge, for instance – this danger was bad enough; far worse was coming downhill where one had less control of momentum, where there was temptation to hurry, even to run or leap, but with the horrifying possibility that one might catch a foot on one of those little stumps, causing a fall headlong down the muddy slope, face first towards sharp protruding sticks.

I always moved downhill with great caution. Some of the boys of my escort would whoop and skip and jump down, and I cringed in fear for their faces if they should tumble. It was noticeable that the true forest-dwellers among the Karen moved through the trees far more cautiously, more quietly, not running at all.

So: one is careful with one's feet in the forest. Never place a foot anywhere that you cannot see. Never go unshod. Never walk carelessly on paths. One can put one's foot in it. In photos of people in forests, they are often gazing upwards at parakeets or acrobatic monkeys – but in truth, those people should be thinking about their feet.

15. FEARS

Since the Karen people began their rebellion against the Burmese government in 1949, they have been slowly but steadily losing. Once they controlled large areas of the country, even threatening Rangoon itself. Today, the Karen Free State is nothing but a few enclaves of territory in the forested hills near the Thai border. Year by year, the huge Burmese army has crept nearer. The Burmese are poor soldiers and badly led – but their numbers are overwhelming.

At the village where I lived and worked with True Love, Bartholomew and the Health Department, the fighting seemed mostly a long way off. But still the war made people nervous and anxious. William was a teacher, headmaster of the senior school and much respected. But his wife, Bella, wanted to go home. She was ten years younger than him. When they had married, down on the Burmese coast, she'd put all her confidence in him. But then he'd brought her to join the Karen rebels. Soon she was terribly homesick and frightened. Like True Love, Bella had not seen her mother for seven years. One day, she set off downriver to a village in the forest near the Front. From there she would send a message to her mother to join her. Bella didn't dare go to the family home near Mergui; she'd be recognised as the woman who'd married a rebel, and would be betrayed by Burmese in the village.

In her absence, William had to run both the school and the family. Day by day, the demands got on top of him, and the children were not cared for. For a while they went regularly to another home for meals. Then William persuaded a teenage girl to come and work as housekeeper. But with their mother gone and the father working all day and half the night, the little children began to run wild.

For weeks there was no word of Bella. Soon, eyebrows were raised. The teenage girl did her best but the house was squalid, the bamboo slimy with spilt rice.

'So, what's new?' said the village gossips. 'Bella was pretty lazy, and stupid too.'

True Love was more sympathetic:

'Bella is young and maybe immature,' he said. 'She's frightened. She fears that she may never see her mother again, and I know exactly how she feels.'

In the meantime, William led the school in the daily oath of loyalty to the Revolution, and organised the military training of the boys. By June, Bella had still not reappeared. William would only say,

'I know where she is; she is safe.'

The gossips began to wonder if she'd ever return, or if there would be a divorce. The young housekeeper moved in full-time, and I often met her carrying the toddlers around the village.

Then we heard news. Bella was simply scared to return, she was terrified of Burmese soldiers. So now her mother came to us, to look after the children. The war was standing the family on its head, and destroying it. And then, one day when I was at a village downriver with True Love and Bartholomew, Bella suddenly appeared, nervous and shy. William, in his quiet way, was overjoyed. The only problem for him was that, to raise cash, he had sold *her* pig to True Love for half the going rate.

Life was growing harder for everyone, and the Burmese began to attack once more, sometimes managing to outmanoeuvre the Karen troops in the jungle. The Karen Army began to show its desperation, recruiting women and young boys. No one was happy about this. No one liked the creeping militarisation now affecting the village. Great Lake didn't like the Army shops that threatened ordinary traders' business. Bartholomew didn't like the military taking over our civilian hospital. The Education chief didn't like his teachers being taken back into the army. Moses the pastor had sleepless nights about his son, a good Christian, who was now at the Front preparing to kill or be killed.

True Love himself was pulled back and forth between competing departments. He became despondent and depressed, concerned for his wife Silver who was pregnant. On one village tour, he suddenly said:

'There is a monastery near here. I would like to visit the monk.'

The monastery was no more than a very small thatched bamboo hut in the forest, in which a single saffron-robed monk sat smoking cheroots and spitting into an enamelled bowl. He and True Love sat questioning each other for half an hour, exchanging news. Then True Love asked if the monk would cast his fortune. The monk drew squares on a piece of paper and began making calculations. His predictions were exact. For the next two years, True Love would be frustrated and passed over for promotion. Then things would improve. In the meantime, he should be exceedingly careful if he got sent to the Front, and beware of his commanders who would not always be the best. And he should watch out for gastric ulcers. In other words, faced with an anxious young officer in battledress sitting cross-legged in his hut, the monk knew just what True Love was worried about.

'It's all just as I thought,' said True Love.

Everyone was affected, even myself. There was a brief rumour that I was a Burmese spy. At the time I was carrying out population surveys.

True Love said:

'Some villagers think you are counting the families in order to reduce their rice ration, and that you will give information to the Burmese.'

I thought that was daft. What could the Burmese want with information about the incidence of miscarriage in Karen villages? But True Love said:

'Many of these people have seen their families hurt and have fled their villages. They have a right to be suspicious.'

After one year, I finally left the Karen Free State. I don't know whether I had done any good. I had trained some nurses, several of whom had promptly got pregnant. I had treated some sick people. I was replaced by a new team from London, but two years later the project folded because of Burmese attacks. As usual, the Karen spotted the enemy coming and evacuated the villages, but they couldn't stop homes being burned, crops destroyed. Many of the villagers fled through the forest over the border and ended up in refugee camps in Thailand.

Some time later, back in Scotland, I received a letter from True Love. He wrote:

> I'm sure that you must have read about Burma in your newspapers. The situation is worse and worse. Students are killed by the government troops. I want to give up all Revolutionary jobs and I want to be a farmer. But Colonel Marvel won't allow me because we have a big problem now.

I wish to be a simple man again.

Hope to see you. With love from

True Love, Silver, and Eddy our little boy.

WHAT DO THEY THINK THEY ARE DOING?

The 'fantastic invasion' of aid workers.

I lived and worked in Java once. I was young, straight out of college and eager to make the world a better place in defiance of Western corporatism. Voluntary Service Overseas was just the thing; I worked in educational publishing in Indonesia, keen to equip Indonesians with the tools and skills to stand up for themselves. Imagine my dismay on receiving a letter from VSO informing me that I was now being sponsored by Jardine Mathieson of Hong Kong, and that I should write and thank them. I had not asked to be sponsored by Scottish colonial capital. I felt betrayed by VSO, and did not write. No more was said.

A few months later, all the British volunteers received a circular from the commercial department of the Embassy in Jakarta. It was a piece of market research, to find out the prospects for various United Kingdom manufactures in Indonesia. We were furious, we burned the questionnaires; we were there to help develop the Indonesian economy, not to assist market penetration by the British. Again, no more was said. Clearly, quite different perceptions of overseas aid were at work in the minds of the sponsors and diplomats – who saw nothing wrong in using young idealists as commercial probes – and of the volunteers, who believed themselves to be on the side of the poor.

One last illustration of the pitfalls for the naïve internationalist: a suggested posting as VSO's field officer in Irian Jaya, the remote eastern corner of Indonesia. This was to be partly funded by the

118

Asia Foundation, in return for our managing a local intermediate technology library. It seemed a splendid idea – until I heard that the Asia Foundation was a front for the CIA and had been kicked out of Malaysia. The volunteer this time would be an unwitting agent of United States policy, as well as of Javanese hegemony in a reluctant eastern province. I began to wonder whether, a hundred years ago, young men from the universities labouring as Assistant District Commissioners in Sikkim, or as medical missionaries in Tobago, ever felt similarly used by the powers of the day. Could one compare the role and attitudes of the administrators of British Indian or Africa with the latter-day aid worker? Why do we wish to be sent abroad? Why does our country ask it?

On my return from Indonesia in 1980, I was recruited for famine relief in Karamoja, Uganda; in a crisis, educational publishing in Java was apparently sufficient experience for emergency nutrition work in East Africa. I enjoyed myself immensely, but was intrigued by my first sight of aid rivalry (the half-dozen agencies in Karamoja squabbled interminably) and also of aid dumping. Some of the international donations were bizarre: we were asked to distribute, to semi-nomadic cattle herders, small tins of fish. More importantly, I witnessed the effects on a local economy of an influx of EC, American and Australian grain. The subsidized farmers of Norfolk and Nebraska did well out of the deal. The farmers of Karamoja saw the bottom fall out of their market through my unwitting agency.

Many workers know their position to be ambivalent. The staff of non-governmental organisations (NGOs) are often highly motivated, well educated and professionally skilled, inquisitive about (and sympathetic to) the cultures in which they find themselves. They would claim, almost without exception, to be advocates for the poor. But they admit that they are tools of diplomacy, international

119

politics and commercial interests. They know, in other words, that aid is a function of what many would call neo-imperialism.

My thoughts on this were brought to a head by encountering Edward Said's *Orientalism* (1978) and *Culture and Imperialism* (1993). Has modern aid work anything to do with Said's gallery of scholars and novelists, with learning and literature as tools for the control of other cultures? There may appear to be little connection between Save The Children struggling to bring high-protein foods to Ethiopian camps and the French linguists dispatched to Napoleonic Egypt. But contemporary aid runs a wide gamut, from medicines and foodstuffs in times of disaster, to British Council (or French, or Australian or Japanese) funding of libraries and scholarships. Bring the graduate students to Keele or Exeter and, with luck, in twenty years' time as an Indonesian government minister, they will buy British and allow us to exploit remote mineral deposits.

The overseas volunteer will initially believe that their field project is less two-faced than this, better calculated to serve and strengthen the developing nation's host community. Then, an uncomfortable realisation may dawn – among, say, some of the battalions of young teachers sent to West Africa, a longtime speciality of VSO – that perhaps the need for rural Ghanaian schoolchildren to learn English is not so pressing as to justify the wholesale undermining of local language and self-respect, that the continual expenditure has more to do with Anglophone cultural hegemony (and the profits of English language publishers) than it has to do with altruism.

Said's thesis – that the investigation and documentation of 'the Orient', its history, languages, religious and material culture, were part of the process of imperial domination – perhaps seems overly portentous when applied to a British Council exchange programme, or the dispatching abroad of linguistics undergraduates for field experience. But the scholars go forth at public expense much as they did 150 or 200 years ago. In many respects, neither the enterprise nor its implications have changed at all.

Missionary scholars have not changed their brief; they do today exactly what their Baptist forebears did in Burma in the 1850s: they run hospitals and translate the Bible. The 'description' of languages by the (Baptist) Summer Institute of Linguistics does not strengthen the victim; the tribal language is unlikely to become a respected tool of administration. Rather, it facilitates penetration and control. There is, meanwhile, a considerable overlap between more dispassionate learning and aid. Many an anthropologist advises on health and educational programmes; of course, aid programmes should be well-informed. But before you know it, the development of a country's schools and health centres, vector eradication and reforestation programmes are dependent on grants and advisers from universities at Vancouver and Tübingen, and a new form of dominion is imposed, doctorate-led.

Overseas aid recruitment is heavily biased towards university graduates, sometimes exclusively so, as in CUSO (Canadian University Service Overseas). Better, runs the argument, to send out people with knowledge to impart, not just another mouth to feed. VSO, Peace Corps and their like are ambassadors, and reinforce the impression that the North is all-powerful because all-knowledgeable, while at the same time our elite gains first hand experience of international relations.

But we may also regards these recruits in other ways: adventurers on behalf of society, in Georg Simmel's meaning of 'adventure': something that occurs on the periphery of our existence, and yet has central importance. Or, perhaps, as the tentacles of our national identity, by which we locate ourselves in the world as it changes around us. There are tensions, of course: narrow pragmatists and bookkeepers may object to these ventures. My own brother, an Amazonian anthropologist, was cited in the House of Commons by Mrs Thatcher as a waste of public money (he's very proud of this). But in general, we adventurers disagree with her. We support the notion that we (our society, not us personally) need to know about, say, changing patterns of pastoralism in the Sahel, and that we should probably be doing something about it, by means of an aid project.

Thus a steady stream of researchers flows from the developed world to the underdeveloped; how much curiosity do we find among the home public for the fruits of all this enquiry? Many an aid worker becomes an author or journalist, well-informed and scathing of just those mismanaged projects they knew at first hand. Such writing, however, has a small, semi-specialist audience. It is curious how little "high" literature has come out of aid. In a world groaning with the intense drama of refugee camps and famine, a tiny handful of plays or novels touch on the subject.

Indeed, the more I have specialised in writing about distant lands, the more I have been forced to recognise that public curiosity is strangely limited. At least, publishers and producers will not risk it unless there is a direct British or American involvement in the story. Hardly a consideration that would have worried the Elizabethans; today, *The Jew of Malta, The Merchant of Venice* and *Tamburlaine the Great* would be stillborn for lack of an Anglo-Saxon lead. I began my own literary career with a play concerning expatriate involvement in Karamoja (Uganda). Fifteen years later, after a spell of covert health work among the rebel Karen of Burma, I wrote a study of this 'ancient society remade for the purposes of ethnic rebellion', which was published by a university press. It was at this time that I read

Said's *Orientalism*. On reading Said, I felt defensive: did my own work follow the patterns he describes? I was in Burma from 1986-87, and my study was published in 1991. Empire was long gone, and the small London health agency was, at that time, funded quite independently of government. And yet we could not free ourselves from the taint of neo-imperialism. Indeed, the Karen frequently invoked their loyalty to British Burma in appeals for our support. From the Karen point of view, our presence merely continued the tradition of missionaries, medics and mercenaries who have muddied Burmese affairs for 200 years with the discreet backing of government. Our work was humane and benevolent; we had no doubt whose side we were on. But we worked with imported allopathic medicines and (partly) in the English language. We may have cured and trained a few, but we also contributed to the weakening of Karen language, skills, identity – or at least, to a remoulding of their traditions into versions acceptable to the late twentieth-century Northern palate, in opposition to the Burmese. American and French mercenaries (and medics and missionaries) were present in the same camps. Who could be sure who was backing whom?

Meanwhile, I gathered notes on the culture. In each overseas post that I have held, some aspects of the project could well be considered naive and/or counterproductive. But, whenever I have become acutely conscious of this, I have also felt that my curiosity and sympathies, firmly with the recipient community, tipped the balance in favour of continued involvement. Again, I wondered if the nineteenth-century scholars dissected by Edward Said ever asked themselves the same questions – and formed the same personal response. Did they, like modern field workers, have doubts? Did they suppress these, or simply learn to live with them?

On occasion, such doubts have burst into the open, famously in 1970 when, at the height of the Vietnam war, the American Anthropological Association split over accusations that field-work among tribes in Thailand and its neighbours Cambodia and Laos, and the funding of the Tribal Research Centre in Chiang Mai, amounted to nothing less than intelligence-gathering prior to annihilation of selected villages by bombing. The Chiang Mai Centre thrives today; indeed, I did some of my own Karen research there Few would now accuse it of scheming genocide. But a suspicion remains that the legions of researchers to be found in the hills of northern Thailand include a good few agents interested as much in narcotics enforcement and strategic intelligence-gathering as in pure scholarship.

Emergency aid has also produced fierce internal critics, for example Alex de Waal. De Waal observed the 1985 food crisis in Darfur (Sudan) at close quarters and wrote an acerbic study of the international response, concluding that the massive effort had saved very few lives (*Famine That Kills,* 1989). His own work was actually funded by Save The Children, a "lead agency" in Sudan which must have had mixed feelings about the published result. But the aid agencies do not give up. When I worked in Darfur's 1991 famine, many of my colleagues had read De Waal's book, yet we went on to repeat many of the mistakes he had identified.

In view of this considerable degree of self-doubt and self-knowledge, it is worth asking, quite literally: What do aid workers think that they are doing? In some quarters, answers such as 'helping' are unacceptable, since they imply a patronizing one-way traffic; one must say 'working together with'. Elsewhere, posing the question in the field elicits responses such as, 'We can at least assist people to regain their hope and dignity', or 'How can we ignore a

124

crisis which is, after all, not of their own making?' These may be honest enough, but while some will acknowledge the role of the World Order in the making of crises, and will readily curse the major international agencies (the UN World Food Programme, the IMF, the World Bank), aid staff are not slow to take powers to themselves. In the title of Patrick Marnham's 1980 book, using a phrase taken from Joseph Conrad's description of the scramble for Africa by European powers in the nineteenth century, aid constitutes another 'Fantastic Invasion'.

As a twenty-six-year-old field officer in Karamoja, I administered much of the food, fuel, communications and non-traditional labour market in a district of 23,000 well-scattered people, if only because the Ugandan authorities were in disarray. In Western Sudan in 1991, our team controlled (if anyone can be said to control anything in Darfur) almost the entire provision of medicines to an area the size of France, and the often excellent local health staff had little choice but to rely on us. In emergency camps in Nepal in 1992, the international agencies and Bhutanese refugee groups ran 50,000 lives with scant reference to the Nepalese authorities. Again and again, the sovereignty of weak countries is undermined by field staff who nonetheless consider themselves advocates for the poor.

To consider aid workers mere hypocrites is, I think, too simplistic. We might, however, examine the history of overseas aid not simply in the light of the White Man's Burden, but of the more ancient springs of charity in society. Charity has frequently (or always?) been a form of control; it may be argued, for example, that the Islamic *zakat* had much to do with buying the political sympathies of the recalcitrant people of seventh-century Mecca. Thus, this particular tool of imperialism is far from new. But still, what is it in our culture that impels us to export highly motivated young people as emissaries in this way? And why do they want to go? These, after all, are not cushy assignments, neither two years as an isolated teacher in a remote bush school, nor six months as a medical worker in a refugee camp. The aid agencies have now realised that psychological distress can be severe among field staff; indeed, in 1992 it was proposed to establish a convalescent retreat in a country house in Devon, especially for returned aid workers. What institutionalised role in the drama of vicarious suffering are the field staff playing for us?

Aid, in its many forms, is today a colossal affair, both in financial and human terms. It is, for the developed North, an institution as solid as was the Victorian poor-box. We consistently direct some 15-20 per cent of our charitable gifts overseas, together now with £25 million of Lottery cash [1997]. We expect our governments to have an aid budget and a responsible minister. We also expect to make a regular offering in the flesh. These fulfil a need in our society to donate, but also represent our engagement with the outside world, an engagement that was once Imperial. There are plenty of studies of the effects on recipient communities. But to understand what is happening, we need a new sociology of concern that embraces the doubts expressed in the writings of Edward Said, while examining the role of aid in donor societies, both the collective traditions and the individual psychology of the emissaries of neo-imperialism.

THE DESERT AND THE RIVER DEE
The fiction of Tayeb Salih and Leila Aboulela

The Sudan, in spite of being Africa's largest country, has always been isolated, whether by vast desert distances or, today, by a vicious and protracted civil war. It is not – as I found, working there for Save The Children in the 1990s – an easy place to live. Communications are miserable. SudanAir's jets are frequently grounded by lack of kerosene or by dust storms, and if you think Railtrack is a mess, try Sudan Railways. In Khartoum, the power fails daily, the water fails, the heat is without pity, the dust gets into everything.

But the country has long exercised a peculiar fascination on the British. Our Imperial sway in the Sudan lasted from the day Lord Kitchener's Maxim guns swept away the hopeless but magnificently courageous 'Dervishes' at the Battle of Omdurman in 1898, to final Independence in 1956. It was rule exercised by a tiny handful of people once characterised as 'athletic public schoolboys' who, unable to play the squire at home, found it fascinating to do so in Africa.

The two writers considered here embody the opposite attraction, the uneasy compulsion that so many Africans have to look to the developed north and to Europe. From their homeland so readily stigmatised as a place of backwardness, oppression, famine, corruption, poverty and almost universal failure, they cannot help but gaze enviously at our wealth and freedoms. Or so it might seem.

But neither Tayeb Salih nor Leila Aboulela is such a simpleton. These are two of the finest writers to come out of modern Africa, and their work scrutinises with great subtlety the strange, chaffing bonds of fascination that bind Europe and Africa.

Tayeb Salih was born in 1929 of orthodox religious and rural peasant stock. He made his way through Khartoum and London Universities to work for the BBC Arabic Service. He is known for just two small books: a short novel – *The Season of Migration to the North* – first published in 1966, and a collection of three stories called *The Wedding of Zein,* both finely translated by Denys Johnson–Davies. This tiny oeuvre has won him a huge reputation with its sophistication and musical poise. The opening of *The Season of Migration* is urbane:

> It was, gentlemen, after a long absence – seven years to be exact, during which time I was studying in Europe – that I returned to my people.

Is that simple word 'gentlemen' not masterly? It immediately conveys culture, a certain power, a worldly self–confidence. One almost imagines brandy and cigars, and the narrator admits: 'I had, in those days, a rather high opinion of myself'. But he is speaking now of a return to a world of poor farmers in 'that small village at a bend in the Nile.' There he is a celebrity, the 'travelled man' whom the villagers bombard with questions about Europe. Is it true that the women are unveiled and dance openly with men? What do they do in winter? Rather to his own surprise, the narrator finds himself insisting of Europeans that, 'just like us, they are born and die... they fear the unknown, and search for love and contentment.'

Even as he holds forth, however, he has become aware of a villager, a man unlike the others. 'That would be Mustafa,' he is told. Mustafa Sa'eed is not a local but a stranger who came, bought a farm and built a house; a man about whom very little is known but to whom the villagers vaguely feel respect is due. After a startling evening when Mustafa Sa'eed suddenly begins to recite First World

War poetry in English, this enigmatic man begins to confide in the narrator – and his story is bizarre.

An orphan, Mustafa Sa'eed was taken under the wing of certain Khartoum British (we are in the era of British rule) who are fascinated by some elusive quality in him and who arrange an education with startling results. Mustafa is clever, perhaps a genius. Soon it is clear that, to fulfil his promise, he must go to study law in London, the London of Bernard Shaw and Edith Sitwell. And now the tragedy begins, as Mustafa becomes entangled with a succession of English women who are as fascinated with Mustafa as he is with England. He lies shamelessly, elaborating his own exoticism. For example:

> Her eyes brightened and she cried out ecstatically:
>
> 'Then you live on the banks of the Nile?'
>
> 'Yes. Our house is right on the banks of the Nile, so that when I'm lying on my bed at night I put my hand out of the window and idly play with the Nile waters until sleep overtakes me.'

The end of this mutual fascination is murderous.

After Mustafa's death, our narrator – back in the village – becomes involved as legal guardian to his widow, an unsophisticated woman who had also been mesmerized by a quality in Mustafa that broke out through the barriers and constraints of rural Sudanese life. A much older man has offered to marry the young widow, his elderly lust dignified by appeal to tradition, for surely a helpless widow should be grateful for his 'protection'. Now the tragedy is replayed – in a scene of truly shocking violence – amongst the Sudanese of the Nile village.

Although Mustafa himself is gone, his influence is still enormously powerful. It is a baleful thing, unsettling those who sense the heady, intoxicating embrace of English and Arab in a far wider world than the villages. It is so strange that the narrator sometimes wonders if Mustafa was real at all: was he not a lie, or a dream all along? Yet he cannot be dismissed, just as the presence of Europe in Africa cannot be undone.

Tayeb Salih's prose is exquisite, even in translation, his descriptions minute and intense. He evokes marvellously the resilience of his people. The narrator says:

> By the standards of the European world we are poor peasants, but when I embrace my grandfather I experience a sense of richness as though I am a note in the heartbeats of the very universe. He is no towering oak tree with luxuriant branches growing in a land on which Nature has bestowed water and fertility, rather he is like the sayal bushes in the deserts of the Sudan, thick of bark and sharp of thorn, defeating death because they ask so little of life. That was the wonder: that he was actually alive, despite plagues and famines, wars and the corruption of rulers.

This is a fascinating, beautiful but, in some respects, an undoubtedly grim novel. Tayeb Salih's novella *The Wedding of Zein* is something quite different, an ostensibly straightforward tale of the loves of the village buffoon. Zein is a 'holy fool' with a capacity for life that triumphs over setbacks. Tayeb Salih's gift for simple but curiously startling observation is everywhere. Here, for example, is how he encapsulates the mentality of the tough peasant farmer:

> Mahjoub lit a cigarette, took two or three pulls, then raised his face to the sky and gazed at it intently, though without

emotion, as though it were a piece of sandy land unsuitable for cultivation.

The presiding sense is one of joy. Here is the wedding itself in full flood:

> Contradictions came together in those days. The girls of 'The Oasis' sang and danced in the hearing and under the very eyes of the Imam. The Sheikhs were reciting the Koran in one house, the girls danced and sang in another; the professional chanters rapped their tambourines in one house, the young men drank in another: it was like a whole collection of weddings. Zein's mother…stopping a moment to listen to the Koran… would then hurry out to where the food was being cooked, urging the women on in their work, running from place to place as she called out, 'Spread the good news! Spread the good news!'

Leila Aboulela – who has acknowledged her own debt to Tayeb Salih – is of a much younger generation and, unlike Salih, she writes directly in English. Resident for some years in Britain, she achieved sudden fame in 2000 when she won the first Caine Prize for African fiction, a prize sometimes called with stunning condescension the 'African Booker', as though an African prize could only be validated as a poor reflection of a European glory. She has gone from publishing in Scotland to Bloomsbury in London, and has been awarded another accolade: serialisation on BBC Radio 4. For a Sudanese woman to come to Aberdeen and win high literary repute is something special.

As with Tayeb Salih, an abiding theme of her stories and of her novel *The Translator* is the unease of the Sudanese expatriate in Britain, the Muslim woman coming to terms with a seemingly cold and godless society, yearning for Africa even while she believes her homeland to have little future.

The Translator is set for the most part in Aberdeen. A young Sudanese woman, Sammar, has arrived there with her medical student husband. In the chilly glitter of the Granite City, Sammar herself finds work as a translator at the university. When her husband is killed in a car accident, Sammar cannot bring herself to return to Sudan. She is prevented by an overwhelming sadness and inertia, a feeling that she would somehow be deserting her husband's memory, and by the hopes and expectations of her family back in Khartoum who have all been banking, literally and metaphorically, on the remittances that the couple would soon be sending home.

In this sorry state, she finds herself slowly drawn towards her Scottish academic boss. This is Rae Isles, a lecturer in politics who specialises in Arab affairs and who is gaining an increasing reputation for an unconventional sympathy with Arab culture and political standpoints. Gradually, a new love develops, but its fulfilment is blocked by the chasm between sympathy and commitment. Rae is an expert on Koranic scripture and modern Islamic writing, its implications for and influence on contemporary politics, including those of terrorist organisations (he would have been much exercised in interpreting Al–Qaeda to the West). Such is his sympathy and understanding that Sammar is perplexed: how can he not become a Muslim? The more he labours to understand and mediate between Arab and European, the deeper his involvement becomes, the more she longs for him simply to speak the words of the *shahadah*, the Muslim profession of faith: 'There is no God but God, and Mohammed is his prophet.'

She longs for this both personally – for then she could with a clear conscience be his wife – and as an African Arab. Just as Tayeb

132

Salih's characters are both fascinated by Britain and in the same instant all the more loyal to something profoundly African, so Sammar knows that in her heart she cannot be anything other than Sudanese, and that for all its apparent hopelessness, there is a quality in Sudanese life and culture that she treasures and will not betray. So at last she returns to Khartoum. And there of course she finds that her family can hardly comprehend her state of mind. For she is now the 'travelled woman', unsettled by all she has seen in that other, European world, and unable to be at ease in either. There in Khartoum she waits for a letter from Rae – and waits, and waits...

Leila Aboulela's Caine Prize was not in fact awarded for *The Translator*, but for a short story, *The Museum*, included in her collection *Coloured Lights*. The story concerns Shadia, a Sudanese woman studying statistics at Aberdeen University, and her unsatisfactory involvement with Bryan, a gauche Scottish student. She is struggling with difficult mathematical concepts in the course; she goes to him for help, and the faint first flickerings of a friendship begin. But, out of her depth and out of her culture, she misplays her hand, saying 'I don't like your earring' and 'I don't like your long hair.' Hardly surprisingly, Bryan walks away.

The attraction remains, however: or is it simply that Shadia is lonely? Again, the African in Scotland – 'where even the fish die of cold' – can hardly feel at home, and yearns for the sunlight of Sudan and the warmth both of African sands and African people. The Aberdeen handbook for overseas students admits that the 'famous British reserve' may be difficult for them, while 'it hinted that they should be grateful, things were worse further south', i.e. in England. And yet, at her back, Shadia's family are not making life easy for her. For while she is raising her defences against the frigid materialists of

Britain, her family are calling on her to buy and ship home every sort of luxury for a new flat in Khartoum:

'I want you to buy fixtures for the bathrooms. Taps and towel hangers. I'm going to send you a list of what I want exactly... You can get good things, things that aren't available here. Gold would be good. It would match...' Gold. Gold toilet seats.

At the same time, some things are curiously back to front. Shadia finds herself surprisingly 'superior' to Bryan. Her father is a doctor, a gynaecologist. What does Bryan's father do?

'Ma' dad's a joiner.'

'And your mother?'

He paused a little, stirred sugar into his coffee with a plastic spoon. 'She's a lollipop lady.'

Shadia becomes startlingly contemptuous.

She said to him, 'The Nile is superior to the Dee. I saw your Dee, it is nothing, it is like a stream...'

Bryan, however, persists in his faintly uncouth, gentle interest in her. Matters come to a head when he proposes a joint visit to a city museum where there is an exhibition about Africa. What she sees there dismays her, for the true subject of the show is not Africa, but Scots in Africa:

The first [exhibit] they saw was a Scottish man from Victorian times. He sat on a chair surrounded with possessions from Africa, overflowing trunks, an ancient map strewn on the floor of the glass cabinet... Her eyes skimmed over the disconnected objects out of place and time. Iron and copper, little statues. Nothing was of her, nothing belonged to her life at home, what she missed

Here was Europe's vision of Africa, the clichés about Africa: cold and old.

The story ends with Shadia weeping and Bryan uncomprehending. But the moral of the tale is complex and subtle. She is angry and insulted and disdainful:

> He didn't know, he didn't understand. He was all wrong, not a substitute. 'They are telling you lies in this museum,' she said. 'Don't believe them. It's all wrong. It's not jungles and antelopes, it's people. We have 7Up in Africa and some people have bathrooms with gold taps…'

Bryan offers hope: 'Museums change. I can change.' When, however, Shadia asks herself if she has the strength to help him change, to guide him on such a journey, she fears she has not that strength. But the question is begged: who is really the more patronising – the intelligent, ignorant but generous spirited European boy of humble origin who offers to try and understand, or the African woman who thinks the project hopeless?

Throughout her writing, Aboulela returns again to such relationships that straddle the uneasy divide between Britain and Sudan. In other stories, Sudanese expatriates return to Khartoum and find themselves visiting British expatriates in Sudan. Or younger people, British Muslims, wrestle with their confused identities and uncertainty about how their culture and religion may continue in Britain. Or they dream and yearn for Sudan and wish they understood how they can both despise its backwardness and yet long to be there. If there is a limitation to Aboulela's writing, it is that this thematic obsession becomes rather repetitive. She writes about little else, and as yet has shown nothing like the imaginative range that Tayeb Salih achieved even in his tiny output; one longs for her to spread her wings.

In her 2005 novel *Minaret,* she does find a new angle on the story. It concerns Najwa, a wealthy, westernised Khartoum girl whose father falls foul of a political coup, and who finds herself come down in the world in exile in London, reduced to working as a maid-servant. In this situation there are many tensions, including the love-hate relationship of an African colony for its former master, but also between rival groups of exiles. Among the Sudanese in London there are victims of other coups, with little sympathy for Najwa's father executed for corruption. There are modernisers, and there are Marxists, but none of these speak to her particular distress. At first she seems carefree, enjoying the shopping and the sights, but as family fortunes dwindle and the news from Khartoum gets worse, Najwa feels rootless, becoming more Sudanese in London than she was in Khartoum.

Only when she comes into contact with the women of the local mosque does she feel touched; the *azan* calls to a hollow in her, she says. *Minaret* is a profoundly Muslim story. Islam comforts and heals Najwa, and it is the Islam of women, relishing situations (without men) when the mood can be 'silky, tousled, non-linear'. The consolations are those of a submissiveness that can be quasi-erotic – she day-dreams of being a concubine – but which is based on renunciation 'when we respect the boundaries of Allah', of wearing the *hijab* and of turning down the love of a younger man to set him free.

Some readers may be irritated by the deliberately narrow emotional range, by an innocence that can seem simplistic, and by a willingness to admit, even to enjoy, naivete and personal limitation. But Aboulela offers these as strengths.

136

What are the qualities of her writing? Her prose moves with the steady pace of someone who knows her faith, and knows she must not falter. She occasionally falters in her English idiom (Najwa takes the chicken from the freezer to 'melt', while an uncle 'immigrates' to Canada) but the writing is often delicate and evocative, as when she describes girls praying out of doors and 'the fall of polyester on the grass,' or when she speaks of a faith that brings 'new gentleness... [as] as all the frisson, all the sparks died away.'

All critics praise her delicacy and restraint. A *Guardian* reviewer wrote of *The Translator*: 'It's a pleasure to read a novel so full of feeling and yet so serene.' Her admirers – who include Ben Okri and J.M.Coetzee – speak of her gentle lyricism. 'She has an unmistakeable style', observed Todd McEwen, 'full of poetry and very moving.'

At the very end of *The Translator* the two protagonists play a game. These (slightly condensed) are the last words of the novel:

> 'We'll give each other thoughts,' he said. 'What did you receive from me?'
>
> I said, 'You gave me silk because of how I was created and you gave me wool to keep me warm.'
>
> Then I looked at what he had received from me. 'Is it perfume?' I asked.
>
> 'No,' he paused and spoke slowly, 'it is something from you that will make me strong.'
>
> When he named it he looked away as if he was shy. 'Admiration,' he said.

Admiration indeed: such is my regard for both these Sudanese writers.

SCOTLAND ON SUNDAY

1. HILLTOP

I come to this column and to Fife by a curious route. I was born to expatriate academics in the Caribbean, expensively but unevenly educated to take a degree in English Literature and Art History which, in the 1970s, did not lead anywhere too clearly. 'Back to the colonies,' said my father, so for a dozen years or more I worked in tropical countries in publishing and 'aid'.

I became a professional dramatist and novelist, and (there can't be so many people who combine these) a paediatric nurse. But I had no home. Afraid that I might end up middle-aged and rootless, I settled in Scotland because I had friends here. And here I have been for some fifteen years: nurse, writer, musician and, now, a husband and a father.

It was my little boy Kit's first birthday yesterday; to show him where (if not who) we are, I take him to the hilltop behind our cottage. From there, just a couple of hundred feet up above the woods, we look over a Scottish panorama. Downstream, we can see the Tay railway bridge and, occasionally, the sun glowing on the tower blocks of Dundee. Upstream, we glimpse Perth. Beyond lies Schiehallion and all the high snowy hills, Macbeth's Dunsinane among them.

On all sides, Kit can see the bones of vanished lives. On the waterfront below us, I point out the fine shell of Ballinbreich castle. Turning west, we have ruined Lindores Abbey and then Newburgh, once home to a linoleum industry that died in the 1970s when the insolvent factory obligingly burned down. Directly over the river is the overgrown Errol airfield; during WWII my father was mistakenly shot down by a Polish RAF fighter stationed there; he survived to ditch in the river. On the near bank is a string of tiny buildings: salmon fisheries, all abandoned now.

The landscape to the south is an array of volcanic plugs and glacial gouging. I show Kit layer on layer of history in ruins. The village is named, I believe, for a Celtic saint. The next hill to the east once had an Iron Age fort. To the south is a dilapidated 16th century tower house now absorbed into a farm. Mary Stuart took tea there, but today the tone is set by a comical concrete silage tower next door, much the same colour as the castle tower and castellated to match.

Next into view comes a decent old parish church. It was once the focus of a *cause célèbre* when parishioners resisted the imposition of a new minister not of their choosing. Black flags were flown from the hills and the poor man's services were boycotted, but those passions are long extinguished; today the church is a private house occupied by an American couple, in business. Right down the centre of the valley there was a railway line serving all the fermtouns to Cupar and St.Andrews, but the line has disappeared. Though the brick piers of bridges that carried the railway over farm lanes are still there, the high embankment is mostly vanished, bulldozed by the farmers. Below me here in our hill's flank is a stone quarry, closed at the end of WWII.

There are farm ruins, too. In each generation, the stronger farmers have absorbed their neighbours, the holdings have grown bigger but the farming population smaller. In a nearby field stands what must once have been a substantial farmhouse, with its own attendant cottages, abandoned in the 1930s. The process continues; of the three farms that abut our little village, one sold off most of its land last year and the other two are up for sale. The village itself, built to house agricultural hands, now has just two men thus employed. My own modest cottage was once three very tiny cottages. My wife, cat, baby and I occupy a space intended for three families. The village is home to people in trades for which town-and-country distinctions have less and less meaning: engineer, builder, retail manager, veterinary nurse, doctor, and a nurse-come-writer. In the heart of the village stands a ruined, roofless doocot.

Looking over this scene, I cannot say to my little boy exactly what it is that we bring, or just how we and the landscape define each other. The only permanent factor is change. Each age built something they thought lasting – fortress, farms, railway, church or quarry – but all have given way. Today, we have the plastic polytunnels of the organic vegetable grower. But we still have some sort of communal identity, and I try to contribute. There is a little school, though numbers are perilously low. We have a hall, and have just won a Lottery grant to renovate it. This is, I think, a lovely place, and I feel blessed to be able to give my boy a home here, wherever it was we came from.

2. REFUGE

In my mind, I lie naked on a string bed sweating my life fluids away, with a desert dust-storm building outside. The reality, however, is that a gale is bashing at the windows of my hut. Outside, the stubble fields of north Fife are drowning.

Evocation is a writer's business, though often we are nowhere near the scene we describe. My friend William Rivière wrote his novel *Kate Caterina*, set amidst the hills of central Italy, in his house on a hill in central Italy, where doubtless oregano scents and olive colours filter into his study. I, however, first drafted my Tibetan story *Blue Poppies* in an apartment block in Los Angeles, describing blizzards while sunlight flickered off the pool. Today, with Fife doing its worst outside, I am in the thick of a new novel set in the burning wilds of Sudan where, a decade ago, I was nursing. I have photos and a pilot's 'operational navigation chart' of Sudan pinned to the wall, and tropical plants in pots. To help my recall, I crank up the gas fire.

I'd long aspired to a writer's hut. Mine's above the garden, on a hillock. I wanted to call it my *refuge de montagne* but my wife objected: refuge from what? It's insulated, double-glazed and features a sloping shelf on which lie three volumes of a massive dictionary, like something in a medieval chained library. I'm well set up – but it's not Sudan, not in this weather.

I've faced this problem before. In the mid-1980s I stayed often with friends on Upper Donside. They'd bought a Victorian shooting lodge and I lodged in the bothy. Then I got a year's work with the Karen, ethnic rebels in Burma, helping them train jungle paramedics. With no other home in Britain I left money for a Donside carpenter to fit my bothy with stairs, windows and electricity. A year later, I returned and moved in; there, a thousand feet up in the Grampians, I wrote a book about the rainforest rebels.

It was a splendid place to work, looking over a burn, with deer-infested forests and Morven (a Corbett) up the track. I found names pencilled on the wooden boards, farm loons who'd lived there, and a date: 1916. But in the winter, in spite of my carpenter's handiwork, the bothy was bitterly cold. I sat inside a sleeping bag with finger-less mittens that allowed me to type. There was an iron skylight with overlapped glass above my bed, and of a morning there would be a little pyramid of snow on my duvet.

The bothy hinted at many things but not Burma, not the malarial forests where for a year I'd occupied a hammock in a bamboo hut. My imagination was taxed.

I was rescued by disease. A month after returning and settling to work, I got a nasty bout of flu, except it wasn't flu, it was malaria. I writhed, sweated and turned about like something in a tumble dryer. By bizarre chance, our GP happened to have a colleague staying, a man who worked in Tanzania and treated malaria every day. Unfazed, they dosed me there in my Grampian bothy. East African malaria being, however, not the same as Burmese, they got the treatment slightly wrong, and a few weeks later, it returned. My friends were away; as I lay in mid-rigor, the phone rang and William was calling from Italy.

He said, 'How are you?'

I said, 'Dying of malaria.'

It's a curious ailment. One day you're racked, the next you're OK, but then the fever returns. The day after this major attack, I drove myself forty miles into Aberdeen in time to have the next bout in hospital. There, I lay remembering the rainforest more readily than before.

Others have been similarly helped. The naturalist W.H.Hudson wrote a wonderful memoir, *Far Away and Long Ago* (1918), recalling his childhood on the Argentine pampas, the sort of book about which connoisseurs nod knowingly. It was composed one miserable, dreich November in a boarding house on the English south coast where Hudson was invalided for weeks, dangerously sick. He wrote:

> On the second day of my illness, I fell into recollections of my childhood. It was a marvellous experience. Propped up with pillows in a dimly lighted room, the night nurse idly dozing by the fire, the everlasting wind dashing the rain like hailstones against the windowpanes; to be awake to all this, feverish and ill and sore, conscious of my danger too, and at the same to be thousands of miles away...

The Fife rain is lashing and bashing my hut just now. I recently received my annual royalty statement from Cambridge University Press for *True Love & Bartholomew: Rebels on the Burmese Border*. The book is, after eleven years, still in print, but it is too expensive; this year they've sold a handful in the USA, and just one here in the UK. In this weather, I hope that one person finds it a warming read.

3. FORTIFICATION

A card comes from France, from friends living near Briançon on the edge of the Ecrins National Park, high up towards the Italian border. They are redoubtable intellectuals in the best French tradition. Andrée once held not one but three chairs at Strasbourg University in psychology and the social sciences, while her husband René, a professor of urban planning, in his retirement went to Sarajevo when it was still under fire to help draw up schemes for reconstruction, and gives his services freely to the shanty towns of Mexico City.

I've visited them since my teens, and once when my wife was pregnant. The landscape is majestic, the Ecrins *massif* topped by glaciers, slashed by gorges and inhabited by chamois and whistling marmots, with teeming flowers, high lakes and scented woods. This is among the warmest regions of France, and Andrée and René (in their seventies) think nothing of rising at five to climb a 3,000 metre peak.

Like many mountainous frontier regions, the area bristles with independence and fortification. In the 14th century the Briançonnais was a semi-autonomous republic astraddle the border. In the 17th, Louis XIV sent his military engineer Vauban to turn Briançon into one of those colossal confections of stonework, ditches and star-shaped bastions that would supposedly hold all Europe at bay – except that (as W.G.Sebald remarks in *Austerlitz*) fortification is often self-defeating, since the grander your defenses, the bigger the besieging army they attract, the heavier the assault artillery.

Within its ramparts, Briançon is a charming, bustling town, the walls littered with sundials. Thirty kilometres down the Durance

144

valley is a rather different castle. Mont Dauphin was also elaborated by Vauban, again to improve its strength against artillery. There was no town within these precincts and when the army pulled out some decades ago, the fortress was deserted. The setting is lovely, and the authorities persuaded artisans to move in; it's now home to the makers of the sundials. For all its massive defences, Mont Dauphin only ever saw one moment of military heroism: in WWII a single Italian aircraft dropped a single Italian bomb, flattening one building.

Twenty kilometres north-east along a narrow gorge is a peculiar stronghold, Fort Queyras, perched on a ledge over the torrent and dating back to at least 1260. The little castle has had a chequered career, burning witches, sheltering princes, besieged in the Wars of Religion and resisting attack by English troops in 1692. Vauban appeared here also, adding his *escarpe, fossé, contre-escarpe et demi-lune* fortifications, but Fort Queyras too was vulnerable to artillery.

Today Fort Queyras is in trouble, privately owned, impoverished and crumbling. The corridors are perilous with rotting floorboards; the balconies have fallen away. In one room, we found a bizarre echo of a different, colder war. Years ago, someone had painted large caricatures of Khrushchev, Kennedy and de Gaulle.

To a Scottish Highlander, the deep forested gorges of the Briançonnais might seem claustrophobic. From the mountain heights the view is forever, but in the valleys one is private and enclosed. For this reason the whole region was once a refuge. The Waldenses were followers of a 12th century merchant-cum-preacher, Peter Waldo, who preached Biblical simplicity, poverty and moral rigour. Such traits don't go down well with the establishment; the Archbishop of Lyons came after him with troops. For centuries the Waldenses were persecuted, with the result that their descendants can now be found from Poland to Uruguay. Many retreated up the gorges of the Briançonnais where for a while they were left alone. But, just as the glaciers on the Massif des Ecrins are gradually shrinking, so the Waldenses' refuge was steadily eroded. The little town of Vallouise, a short walk from Andrée and René's house, is named after King Louis XI who in 1486 put a brief stop to the persecutions, but these soon recommenced. Walking up the lovely secluded valley of the Torrent de Celse Niere, Rona and I passed a spot marked as a place of execution, where Waldenses who had been caught by Royalist soldiers died as martyrs in the purity of their faith.

On our wedding anniversary, September 11th, we took Andrée and René out to a good lunch at Embrun, near Mont Dauphin. I asked René more about the Waldenses: what had happened next? He shrugged: more massacres. At home after lunch, gravid and tired, Rona lay down to rest. Moments later, René tapped at the door, calling me upstairs, ostensibly to consult about computing. It was a ruse. He wanted me to see the television news, but was concerned that the shock might do Rona harm. The artillery was winning again. On the screen – repeated over and over – we watched young men from an international quasi-religious group die as martyrs in the purity of their faith, by flying jumbo jets into the sides of tall buildings.

4. KEITH

My father-in-law, Jim, is in the grip of an obsession with a man not half his age. Thankfully, the latter died in 1879. His name was Keith Johnston and he'd been sent by the Royal Geographical Society of London to find a route from Dar-es-Salaam to the Central African lakes. He never made it; like dozens of other young explorers, Johnston died of dysentery. Unlike Livingstone, no one lugged his eviscerated carcase back to Britain, and he's been largely forgotten.

A few years ago, however, his dusty calf-covered diary resurfaced at the Royal Scottish Geographical Society in Glasgow, and Jim settled with a magnifying glass to transcribe the minutely spidering scribble. He showed us pages as he worked: a surveyor's log of the 'walked thirty yards south, then turned seventy yards east' variety, scattered with fragments of Swahili. The diary itself is not a riveting read.

But the circumstances of the expedition are intriguing and poignant, and Jim began to research Keith's Johnston's background and family. By extraordinary chance, he discovered Keith's great-niece living a few minutes walk away in Edinburgh, and she had two volumes of family letters and *Recollections* written by Keith's sister Grace, author of Victorian bodice-rippers. The archive brought to life the world of 19th century Edinburgh cartography, the rival firms of W. & A.K Johnston and Messrs Bartholomew, the missions and the high imperial ideals.

My mother-in-law Jill began to feel that someone had moved into the house as, like scabies, Keith Johnston got under Jim's skin. It must be partly to do with certain coincidences. Jim retired a few years back from top management at the Scottish Nature

Conservancy, but he started out as a backstreet loon in Dundee, battling his way to the top of school. He had sat, one day, perched like Oor Wullie on a log in a wood and decided he wanted to be a forester. First, though, National Service found him as a teenage officer in the Black Watch, seconded to the King's African Rifles in Kenya at the time of the Mau Mau rising. Some years later he returned to Africa as the first white post-graduate student at Makerere University in Uganda, sent there with a Leverhulme scholarship and the bizarre instruction to help the African students with their hobbies, to broaden their horizons.

In 1961, Jim became a forestry officer in Tanganyika, tasked with mapping a forest through which a proposed railway could run. This was in the Selous Game Reserve, exactly the area that Keith Johnston, in the 1870s, was surveying for a first trade road between the coast and the central African lakes. The routes of Johnston's road and Jim's railway actually touched. Jim read Johnston's descriptions of crossing rivers in dugout canoes, paddled by natives and clutching his rifle. Delighted, Jim produced a photograph of himself as a forestry officer, ninety years later, crossing those same rivers in a dugout canoe, paddled by natives and clutching his rifle.

For a couple of years now, Keith Johnston has ruled my in-laws family home. He pops up at every meal, as Jim excitedly reveals another link he's discovered in the archives. In 2001 he got a new notion: he'd retrace Johnston's route. Jim set off with Mike Shand, a Glasgow University cartographer, to find Behobeho, the village where Johnston expired, and to locate the grave. They had a German map of 1900 that showed the village, a GPS device and a description of the burial by Joseph Thomson, Keith's young assistant. And they knew that in *c.*1890 the Johnston family had dispatched a tombstone, shaped like a desk and made of Swedish granite. It took 100 men almost a year to carry this from the coast.

Jim never found it. He and Mike Shand floundered through mud and vicious serrated grasses, were chewed by tsetse flies and harassed by hippos. But of the monstrous tombstone there was no sign. Perhaps the river had changed its course. Perhaps the thing had simply sunk into the soft earth under its own weight. Mike Shand, now also obsessed, went back next October with a bigger expedition and a better GPS, and still couldn't locate it.

What on earth drove young men like Johnston, one after another, to set off into that bush, knowing that the mortality rate was so appalling? The example of Livingstone? A rage for reputation? Few of the Victorian African explorers escaped severe illness. Jim reached home amply scratched and bitten but nothing worse. He'd found conditions for bush travel hardly changed; the big difference is the availability of modern medicines.

He's now burying himself in 'son of Johnston', the tale of William McEwan, another young Scot similarly engaged in road surveying just five years later, and almost as quickly dead. Jill sighs patiently, and prepares to make room for another Victorian ghost moving into the family home.

5. RENDITIONS

Next week, my novel *Blue Poppies* is published in the USA. Putting my work into foreign hands is an exciting if sometimes alarming process. The New York publishers, Bantam Dell, insisted on the right to 'Americanise' the text as required, and I almost took fright. I've no objection to spelling changes (I can't spell anyway) but what if they made my Scottish character sound like a boy from Brooklyn? In fact, the US publishers have behaved impeccably over this, and if anyone is tempted by cheap prejudice regarding American literacy (or its lack), they should sample the attentions of a New York copy editor: the minutely detailed enquiries, the scrupulously documented emendations always justified by a note in the margin, all paid tribute to a rigorous strand in US education.

As a rule, I rather like being edited: who else but an editor would take my prose so seriously? Once in a while, the Americans startled me. Vocabulary they wanted altered included 'col' (as in mountain) which they claimed they couldn't find in their dictionaries, which also declared 'shambolic' to be a 1970s coinage of limited currency. Saki's lovely word 'studge' (for a glutinous gruel) had to go; I suppose few Americans read Saki. But I've hung onto 'hoiked'.

The experience was quite different with the Greeks; a Greek translation is also just out, and I have sample copies. It looks very handsome, but not only can I not read it, I cannot even make the sounds that the Greek letters represent. I can't check any aspect of the translation; for all I can tell, the first sentence could be wildly (perhaps gloriously) obscene. I expect they've done me proud, but I take it on trust that this is in fact my novel.

At various moments in literary history, all sorts of things have been blamed on innocent authors. In the late 17th Century, pornographic verse was imported from the Netherlands and ascribed to the Earl of Rochester, who'd had rather a reputation that way. Around 1500, Venetian printers turned out endless musical junk marketed under the name of Josquin des Prez, knowing that Josquin always sold and the great man would soon be dead so who cared.

Early translations are often less accurate but more spirited than later, more scholarly renditions. The liveliest version of *Don Quixote* is Pierre Motteux's of 1720, even though Motteux liked to add his own jokes. A new Penguin edition of Proust is out; its correctness cannot disguise occasional lumpish pedantry, compared to the old Scott-Moncrieff. *The Way by Swann's* may be more exact than *Swann's Way* as the English for *Du Côté de Chez Swann* but I know which I prefer. If anyone wants to translate Falla, I hope they remember to enjoy themselves.

Some years ago, my play *Topokana Martyrs Day* was translated into German. The translator was baffled by one word, a reference to a portable radio. He wrote to ask whether 'tranny' was an error or a common abbreviation of 'tyranny'?

Topokana also made it onto BBC World Service radio, and now there entered a new consideration in playing to distant audiences. The producer phoned me:

'I hope you won't mind. In deference to Asian and African sensibilities, we've cut the naughty bits.'

'Oh.' I thought a moment. 'Which naughty bits?'

'Well, your original ran for just over two hours. We're down to one hour.'

The irony was that the play is set in Africa.

I'm delighted to think of my work creeping out into the wide world. I like to imagine quite different cultures finding some use for it. Doing my accounts, I came upon a credit note for royalties due from a film I wrote for the BBC. It informed me that *The Hummingbird Tree* had been broadcast in Argentina and Poland. What a lovely thought. Were the broadcasts simultaneous? As the final credits rolled, did my fans in Buenas Aires rush to telephone their cousins in Wrocław to compare notes?

I have, infrequently, been the translator. I briefly earned my olives in Venice by translating for a little tourist magazine, *Un Òspite da Venezia*. In 1997 I was interpreter for a joint production by Nicaraguan and Scottish actors at Robert Rae's Theatre Workshop. I was stunned to find how little my bad Castilian corresponded to Nicaraguan actor's argot, but we won a Fringe First nonetheless. Occasionally I've translated poetry from Italian or Spanish, just for fun. Here's a medieval Spanish lyric, in the Falla version:

> As I walked by your doorway
> The lemon you threw made me start.
> The lemon rolled into the gutter,
> But the pain went straight to my heart.

The copyright world is changing now, and the Writers Guild tell me not to be so carefree. If I am not vigilant, media ghouls will steal my work, render it into Hokkien and disseminate it worldwide in unforeseen formats; I may resurface on a Gameboy. 'Bless thee, Bottom,' wrote Shakespeare, 'thou art translated.'

6. SHOOTIST

The woods behind me ring with gunfire. With luck, there'll be a brace of pheasants on the coal bunker by evening, courtesy of a neighbour. Our leaders and media are hotly debating firearms control and gun culture. How might I fit into gun culture when it comes for me? What style or persona should I adopt? I've considered the following.

The gentleman: I have gentleman friends who have guns. One even has a gun room, with rifles and shotguns of different calibres in a locked cabinet. I have the posh education, I have the accent, I'm not a bad shot. But I loathe dogs.

Wild Man of the Marshes: I've been told that our little Fife town nearby has the highest per capita gun ownership in the UK; it's to do with traditions of wildfowling in the Tay reedbeds. The word 'wildfowling' puts me in mind of pub engravings, of rustics in waistcoats lain full length in rowing boats, poking long muskets at ducks. I'm a decent shot – but I detest being cold in boats.

Old Safari hand: I did myself once own a gun. It was an ancient double-barrelled twelve-bore and it had belonged to the Bishop of Mombasa, Kenya (his name was in the leather case). Instead of a locked wooden cabinet, I kept it under my bed. I would set out after the rabbits of Oxfordshire, stalking them on the grassy slopes of the reservoir. I'm rather a good shot, truly, and once hit two rabbits with a single discharge. My friend William refused to be impressed and claimed that they'd been tied together to a tree, like Roosevelt's teddy bear. Another friend who was staying with me fainted when I began to gut the rabbits and we found tapeworms.

Master of Self-sufficiency: I moved to Aberdeenshire and took the Bishop's Bazooka with me. We had a teenage German to stay, a nice boy. He wanted to shoot so we went after rabbits. I carefully instructed and guided him to a vantage point from which he killed a small animal. He was tremendously proud of this, but something in his eyes afterwards I found thoroughly off-putting.

The Bishop's gun was also employed to execute a neighbour's goat for the freezer. It was a young billy, useless for milking but pretty. As we were tying it up, it started to suck my fingers as though my hand was its mother's teat. I don't think I ever used the gun again, and sold it to the local policeman for £20.

The Conservationist: I once hunted big game to preserve the balance-of-nature. That was in Java, when another local policeman invited me to go after wild pigs in the forest because they'd been terrorizing village gardens. Before setting out, to ascertain my prowess, this policeman set up a straw basket in the yard. I'm a good shot, I tell you, I blew that basket away. We rose before dawn and crept about in the mountain undergrowth but never saw the pigs, let alone killed one.

Reluctant Man of Action: Goats, guns and police are a potent mix. I've been shot at twice, both of them in Uganda. In 1981 I was working for Oxfam, and was the boss of a remote field outpost. I had a flock of four goats providing milk and edible offspring. Those were lawless, hungry times. One night the air was split by automatic rifle fire, some of which smacked through the window and into the wall of my bedroom. My watchmen and I took prudent cover, and in the morning we found that the goats were gone. However, their tracks were clear. The watchmen followed these, returning to report that they led to the police station. We hesitated – but thankfully bail was granted: at least, three of the four goats wandered their own way home that afternoon.

Gangsta. A few years ago my family gathered at my parents' house in Wiltshire. On Christmas Eve, my stepfather (not a young man) remarked that he'd found a pistol in the attic, and had put it back. We stared at him, until I fetched a ladder, opened the hatch and groped under the fibreglass insulation. I came down and held out a small automatic.

'No,' said my stepfather, 'that's not it.'

We stared again; I climbed back up. This time I came down with a much bigger automatic, a black Colt.

'That's it,' he smiled.

My brother and I drove off into the night. I was wearing a black leather jacket and had both pistols tucked inside. We entered Devizes police station, ready to cross-draw and scream defiance. We'd have fallen in a hail of crossfire but they'd have paid, my God, I'm really quite a shot! As it was, a WPC said, 'Oh right, thank you,' took the pistols and dropped them into a cardboard box under the counter. She didn't even ask if I had terrorist affiliations. I was very disappointed.

Such are my essays at gun culture.

7. EXTREMADURA

We're off to Spain, our first trip abroad with baby Kit. I feel possessive about Spain, based on a conviction that I discovered the country, *circa* 1965. My older brother was an anthropology student and for him the trip was 'field work'. The family tagged along, though my grandfather was sceptical; he said Spaniards turned green when they grew old.

The past is another country, wrote L.P. Hartley; they certainly did things differently in old Spain. For centuries, the country had a grim reputation known as the Black Legend, an image enthusiastically promoted by Spain's enemies and compounded of the Inquisition and the slaughter of American Indians, of Velazquez dwarfs, gloomy palaces, Goya's *Horrors of War*, and miserable poverty in a parched landscape. Franco's Spain lived up to this image. In 1965 we motored south in my mother's blue Renault R4, passing through Burgos; that was where the General kept his political prisoners. I remember hoping we'd avoid the prison, and wondering if we'd hear tortured screams as we drove by.

We headed for a village in the Sierra de Gata, the Cat Mountains in the Extremadura close to the Portuguese border. Luis Buñuel made a film here called *Land Without Bread* (1931), a surrealist documentary in which the human condition is so awful that it becomes comic. Our village derived its income from oranges and from smuggling political refugees out of Portugal (then ruled by the dictator Dr Salazar) over the mountains and north to France. Even the goats and donkeys looked poor. The steep lanes were of dirt and rock; farm animals lodged in the ground floor byres. Our diet consisted of bread and onions, Three Candles chocolate – a confection that resembled

156

Scotbloc blended with sand – and goat meat. The latter, at least, was very fresh. One batch we brought back to our lodging was, when we opened the brown paper, still twitching.

We lodged in two rooms over a bar called The Oranges. The bar (which was indeed crammed with sacks of oranges) sold little but sour red wine and soda, served by an urchin called Julian. Tucked in one corner was the only sanitation for the whole household. The village seemed to be run by the Catholic clergy. We went to mass one Sunday; I can still hear the priest in his pulpit high over the dark, crowded nave thundering at his flock, 'The Church is your future!' We were made welcome everywhere, and were very happy. I returned a few years later, hitching by myself aged 16, and have headed back to Spain frequently ever since. Now I hope to sell it to Kit.

Spain, back then, had a rotten name throughout the rest of Europe. No one would touch anything tainted by Franco; even today I have elderly left-wing friends who will not go to Spain. In the sixties and seventies, holidays there were either for the very rich with apartments in an exclusive little seaside resort called Torremolinos, or for the proletariat who knew no better.

As a child I was taken to an embarrassing Adam Faith film, a so-called comedy entitled *What a Whopper* (1961). The story concerned the Loch Ness monster, but one character owned a concession for a make of Spanish cars called Bella: they were ugly, cheap and wouldn't start. The very notion of trying to sell Spanish cars labelled this man a fool and a loser. Spanish wine was dreadful too, and for years no one would buy Spanish olive oil, so it was secretly shipped to Italy and re-branded.

Not all of that bad old Spain has gone. They are, just now, digging up the mass graves from the Civil War. The south still has its poverty, the result in part of vast landholdings dating from the 15th century, such that a very few families own a high proportion of the land, keeping seasonal labourers on low wages.

But otherwise the transformation is astonishing. Forget Bella cars: today, 65% of SEAT cars are exported and Spaniards sit in top management at Volkswagen. Forget Torremolinos: in Cupar, Fife, we've an estate agent dealing solely in Spanish property. The country thrives, is hospitable, courteous and fun. The trains are much better than Britain's and the circle of friends we now visit in Andalucia are busy middle-class professionals who are… well, just like us. Extraordinary!

My brother is planning a forty-year reunion in the Extremadura. Recently he revisited the village. It was neat, paved and, if not prosperous, certainly presentable. Four decades on, they remembered him. Back in Cambridge, he received an email out of the blue: someone had tracked him down through the Internet. It was Julian, the urchin who had once served the coarse wine in The Oranges Bar. He's now an IT expert based in Madrid.

8. REKINDLINGS

One February weekend three years ago, with snow threatening, I spent two days in a pretty but icy little church south of Edinburgh, evoking the burning south of Spain in song. We were making a recording, 'we' being Fires of Love, the Early Music quartet I work with.

It was so cold that we sang dressed in coats, woolly hats and mittens, only taking these off when required to play an instrument. To keep my recorders in tune, and to prevent the curling metal mouthpiece of the bass recorder filling with condensed spit faster than a Glenfiddich still, I stood directly over an electric fire, trying to hold the instrument in the warm updraft as I played. Our lutenist blew onto his fingers, our drummer fretted over his chilly skins, our soprano shrank into her mufflers. Out in the porch, the Delphian Records engineer groaned as a frigid dew settled on his expensive and sensitive DAT machines. Hardly ideal conditions for a programme of music from Andalucia called 'Love & Reconquest'. When we'd finished, we got out by the skin of our teeth. A blizzard was blowing, the lanes were filling with snow. Back in Fife two hours later, I drove into a drift and stuck.

Such are the pleasures of Early Music in Scotland. It's an under-developed market. For three years we'd been plying our trade around the country, jammed into my rusting Toyota with a roof-box as long as the car to accommodate drums and an elongated archlute, performing to local music societies from the Borders to the far west coast, earning a professional fee when we could, covering our costs at least. We refused to wear codpieces, and tried to insist that our repertoire was as mainstream as Bach. We did some awful things to keep afloat, including two gigs for international conferences. One was for a pleasant but bemused bunch of electronics experts in Edinburgh castle, where we found ourselves in direct competition with a punk bagpipe ensemble and a falconer. The falcon buggered off in disgust and, after a while, so did we.

Audiences were, to begin with, apprehensive and sceptical. In one Borders town, we tuned up in a little modern theatre and played a trial song.

'How does that sound?' we called to a committee member lurking at the back.

'All right,' he muttered, 'if you like that sort of thing.'

I have a passion for that sort of thing, for Renaissance secular music, the songs of Josquin and Narvaez, Willaert and Dowland, the soundtrack of Shakespeare's plays and the operas of Monteverdi. With two voices, two lutes, and lots of guitars, recorders and drums, there wasn't much we wouldn't tackle. Our touchstone for authenticity was: I'm sure at the time they'd have worked with whatever resources were to hand.

I also adore the texts. Some of my happiest days have been spent in libraries tracking down ancient lyrics. I've stumbled on the original of a 17th century Roman lullaby in a Neapolitan song of the early 1400s. I've worked out that *Durandarte* does not refer to the Carolingian hero Roland, as usually claimed, but is instead a strange personification of Roland's sword (see me for details). I've come up with many an unsubstantiated theory and I'm sticking to them all. I've sweated cheerful blood over translations. Some songs are settings of super-refined and near-impenetrable Petrarch sonnets. Others are anything but refined: occasionally, even I blink at the ribald texts. One Venetian song openly incites youth to beat up old

160

ladies in the piazza, for obstructing young love. The chorus urges, 'Beat them! Beat them with sticks!' It never fails to get a nervous laugh.

We had Lottery money for equipment, we had classy design work done, we had some splendid reviews (well, mostly) and had played abroad (well, England, lodging on the floor of a nursery school). But it all fell apart. In the best rock-and-roll manner, just as we were about to launch our CD, we quarrelled. We patched our differences for the launch night... and that was that. I had to cancel ten concert engagements.

We've not worked as a quartet for eighteen months since, although the rump three of us have kept a small flame alive. Our problem has been replacing our lutenist. As I said, it is a small and under-developed field. England has its National Early Music Centre in York, innumerable ensembles and a score of festivals. Scotland has not one; professional lutenists north of the border may be counted on one hand, all spoken for.

Imagine our excitement on just now catching wind of a new arrival: an expatriate Scottish lutenist, returned to the Lothians. We've snaffled him for Fires of Love before any one else can. The Renaissance repertoire ranges from the whacky to the sublime, and it's possible that we give some pieces their first Scottish performances in hundreds of years. That alone lends a sense of mission.

[Note: In the event, we fell out with the new lutenist also, and were relieved and delighted to make friends with the old one again.]

9. CREOLE

A publication this month gives me particular pleasure, although it won't set the Frankfurt Book Fair alight or make the *Scotland on Sunday* review pages. It is a cheap paperback reprint of the second edition of a dictionary of English as spoken in Jamaica. I've three reasons for my pleasure.

Firstly, simple pride: it's a work of enormous scholarship and my father wrote it, together with American creolist Fred Cassidy. In the early 1950s, my father Robert was a young lecturer at the new University of the West Indies (where I was born). He taught Anglo-Saxon poetry, finding that Caribbean students better understood the harsh realities of life behind the poems than did many British undergraduates. Robert remembers how intelligently a young poet named Derek Walcott (the future Nobel winner) read *Beowulf*.

In the 50s, investigation of creoles had barely commenced; who'd want to study bad language? But Robert was intrigued to find that he could understand little of the English that working-class Jamaicans spoke to each other. *The Gleaner*, Jamaica's newspaper, had in 1943 run a competition for 'the best list of dialect words and phrases' and he was given the original entries, many of which were charming, for example:

Gonorear: gentleman complain.

So began the *Dictionary*. For some thirty years, Fred and my father collected and researched across the Caribbean. In the early days they had a clockwork tape-recorder, and sat under trees with storytellers and bottles of rum. They also sent out questionnaires modelled on the Scottish Dialect Survey, just then being published. Research could get

162

you into trouble; Robert was thrown out of one Trinidad hotel when the manageress saw him take two black boys into his room for unspeakable acts (very speakable, actually: they were story-tellers, and he had his tape-recorder in there). There were letters to the press, denouncing him for shaming the island by drawing attention to the corrupt English of the ill-educated. But he and Fred persevered, with Cambridge University Press publishing the first edition of the *Dictionary of Jamaican English* in 1967.

A second reason for pleasure: the *Dictionary* is delightful, is fascinating. It is an encyclopaedia of Caribbean life, work, witchcraft, song, food, history, botany (recording the local names of scores of plants), even transport: a chi-chi is a bus named after the sound of its air brakes. Jamaican creole-English derives in part from the languages of West African slaves and of Indian indentured labourers, and draws heavily on French, Spanish and Scots: many of the island's traders, sugar estate managers and latterly doctors were Scottish. 'Scotch grass' is a species originally imported from a district of Barbados called Scotland. 'Scotch attorney' is a parasite, a sort of vine that grows upon other trees until they are strangled.

Fred and my father spent years hunting after precise meanings, and were sometimes defeated. The old competition entries were often from people of limited schooling, and for some items the *Dictionary* can offer no definition but the words are included nonetheless, because they meant something to someone, and one day we may discover what. How many academics have that sort of intellectual humility?

The etymologies they traced demonstrate what really happens with words, which is not what certain grammarians, structural theorists and purists assert. There's a fruit tree in Jamaica called by country people the 'cherry-million' tree, because of the profusion of small cherry-like fruits that it bears. But the original name of the

163

transplanted tree was the Malay 'chermai', nothing to do with cherries or millions. Jamaicans heard the newcomer's name, saw the fruit and drew their own conclusions. That is how language develops, not because National Academies, 'deep-structure' theorists or newspaper letter columns lay down laws.

Dictionaries like this, and creole studies generally, are profoundly humane. Creoles teach us to look at the lives of common people, to understand how the pressures with which they cope govern how they speak. The poor – whether in the Caribbean or in Scotland – do not speak a poor language, a disordered, ungrammatical version of the speech of the elite. Rather, it is the elite who are fools if they imagine that there is such a thing as 'correct' language that corresponds wonderfully to their own. If we would remember that English is, in large part, a mixture of barbaric German and bad Latin (i.e. French) we might be a little less dogmatic. Creoles have a great deal to tell us.

The third reason for my pleasure is the fact of the cheap reprint. The CUP editions of 1967 and 1980 were finely produced but very expensive; the Dictionary cost £80; few in the Caribbean could afford it. But at last it is to be issued by the University of the West Indies Press at a lower price. Thus, in one very small sense, Jamaican English goes home. Last year the University gave my father an Honorary Degree. Now very frail, he attended a thanksgiving by satellite link. I hope you will pardon my pride.

10. PATAGONIA

This month, December, is the season for visiting Patagonia. I've been judging a short-story competition, one of the strongest entries being set in a prison on Tierra del Fuego, and it takes me back. There, the days are long just now, and the sun warm. It is strange to enter a succession of long-haul jets and transfer lounges, emerging thirty hours later on the Magellan Straits, a journey that took Magellan himself more than a year of sailing into the unknown. My wife and I stood on the foreshore at Punta Arenas, gazing at Tierra del Fuego across the water. At our backs was a windswept little funfair. Bored Chilean conscripts rode the ghost train, then boarded a huge mechanical ship which swung them giggling to and fro in the chill air.

The ship attraction was called *¡Pirata!* – perhaps referring to Francis Drake. Our great circumnavigator is known in Chile for a pirate and a murderer; in August 1578 he initiated the gross violence against the native peoples that continued until their extermination by European sheep farmers. On Tierra del Fuego in the late 1800s the chief culprits were a Prussian, Jakob Popper, and a Scot whose name is recorded as Mr McInch, a man who systematically slaughtered the Fuegians, reputedly being paid *pro rata* for the ears collected.

In Punta Arenas, Chile's southernmost city, the houses are clad in tin sheets, like beached gunboats. It has been described as a blend of Dar-es-Salaam and Aberdeen, a fresh and friendly place. Our first evening in a café, my wife and I were both kissed on the head by an amiable drunk, while another diner offered his warm condolences for the death of Princess Diana, 'which greatly affected us here'.

What of those contentious islands out in the Atlantic?

'We don't call them Falklands,' he said, 'we call them the Malvinas.' The name Malvinas is neither indigenous nor Spanish but Hispanicized-French; the islands were named by a visitor from St Malo.

The grandest edifices are in the cemetery and again Scots are prominent: *Duncan Macleod, born Stornoway 1880, died Punta Arenas*, and many others. It's easy to see what they came for: huge tracts of land, empty (natives apart) and ideal for sheep, a scene very like Lewis only a thousand times larger, with vast open skies and winds to make a Hebridean feel at home.

In place of gannets there are colonies of Magellanic penguins. Some derive the name from the prosaic Welsh *pen gwyn* ('white head'), but the cheerful Latin *pinguitudo* ('fatness') is surely preferable; Latin fatties is what they are. It's the women who rule the penguin colonies. The males stand about in feckless groups until picked by a girl who takes a pebble and drops it wherever she requires her beaux to dig a burrow. Drake's men killed 3,000 of them for food.

Such terrain demands courage and hard work, and is unforgiving. In 1584, to forestall the English, Philip II sent fourteen ships and 4,000 men to establish a Spanish presence on the Straits. Only 300 arrived and, when they finally lost their last ship in a storm, they were doomed, starving to death or hanging themselves in despair. For centuries, the numerous and fierce Araucarian people resisted Spanish and German colonists, and today Chilean and Argentinian Patagonia preserves a reputation for proud liberty. The local spirit was never quite crushed either by Pinochet or Galtieri, and there are moving tango songs extolling the 'dignity' of the South. Indeed,

Chilean Patagonia is entirely cut off by rock, ice and water. To reach the north overland, you must cross into Argentina and back.

We were there for the mountains and the walking. A day to the north of Punta Arenas, out of the level pampas rises the Torres del Paine, a geological wonderland. Vertical towers of basalt 1,000 metres high jut up alongside a vast glacier. Guanacos (small llamas) trot about the surrounding plains, condors sail black against the gleaming sky and families of silver foxes play among the rocks, quite disregarding the hikers. There are rheas, ibises, even parrots. Wild flowers sprout in a hurry, for the season is short.

The Torres del Paine, now a well-run National Park, is a very long way from anywhere, but its isolation has been eroded. Each summer, 50,000 visitors arrive, many of them young Israelis out of college and into globe-trotting; I picked up a discarded gas lighter with a label in Hebrew. The weather is more congenial to Scots than Hebrews; it changes every five minutes, veering from sunshine to blizzards and back.

There are refuge huts, but we carried heavy packs with everything for a week's camping, the load such that, concluding each meal, we would calculate the grammes of food thus taken off our shoulders. We pitched one night on a black beach; in the morning, icebergs floated past our tent.

All this comes back to me in Fife, as I sift through the story competition hopefuls.

11. DECLAIMING

I've had a courteous enquiry asking if I'd like to be involved in running a poetry festival. I wish them well, but have declined. I long ago had my fill of organising poets, and have only slowly come to enjoy readings once more.

I wrote youthful verse myself. At college I fell in with enthusiasts and we founded the Cambridge Poetry Society. In the 1970s readings were subsidised by the National Poetry Secretariat. We'd book a poet, pay them £20 and the NPS would match that with another £20.

We flourished, we were eclectic. Basil Bunting came, elderly and stiff but wonderfully sonorous reading *Briggflats*. Hugh Sykes Davies, venerable surrealist, demonstrated voice amplification: I don't recall his exact thesis, only that he said, 'Open voice, closed voice', over and over, moving a microphone to or from his lips.

J.H.Prynne remarked to him afterwards, 'Hugh, I could listen to you reading a bus ticket with pleasure.'

Steven Srawley played us his electronic-montage piece based on Charles Tomlinson's lovely poem, *I have seen Eden*; I still treasure the vinyl. We got Christopher Ricks to lecture on the lyrics of Bob Dylan, and made a fortune at the door. We screened avant garde films by the American Stan Brakhage (lost a bit on that) and held a symposium on 'the new poetries', visually treated texts and 'sound poems' (a nett financial gain).

But there were tensions. Some of my associates were hard line about the future of the art. For me, the finest reader was Richard Murphy

168

whose gentle voice made music from the understated but exquisitely delicate rhythms of *The Maisie*. Not all my colleagues approved. Two of the Committee, sitting in the front row, ostentatiously stood and walked out, with all the self-importance of Ulster Unionists leaving peace talks. Murphy smiled after them bemusedly.

Indeed, the only way I'd persuaded the Committee to invite Murphy at all was by a scam whereby we'd pay him the NPS part of the fee but not our own. Murphy, sweet-natured soul, had agreed, but I wince with shame to remember our handing him a cheque for £40 and then asking for £20 back.

In 1975 another poet, Richard Burns, launched the Cambridge Poetry Festival, and I was drawn in. It was a grand and glamorous affair. Ted Hughes was our patron, large grants were obtained, the greats of modern verse received their invitations and quite a few obliged. The Cambridge audience was not easily impressed, however, and were merciless to poor readers. John Ashberry sat at a desk in the debating chamber of the Students Union and mumbled incomprehensibly. After half an hour, there was the strange spectacle of this distinguished and highly influential American being heckled by poetry aficionados, many of whom owned all his books.

There were parties and concerts, and poster-poems which had recently become fashionable. One of these was a love poem beginning *It is very nearly morning*, printed over a grainy photograph of a lovely post-coital girl naked and pensive with her knees drawn up. Unfortunately, the thought occurred to me that it resembled an advertisement for a feminine intimate deodorant, and I couldn't look at it.

Why did I come to dislike readings? Basil Bunting wrote: Poetry lies dead upon the page, until some voice springs it to life. But after a year or so, I couldn't escape the conclusion that too many poets read their own work terribly poorly. Too many affected a dour disdain for anything resembling confidence, and read in a tone of wan self-effacement in which almost every line was given a lugubrious rising terminal, as though they all came from Liverpool.

There were always, of course, exceptions: Pushkin could reduce salons of stuffy Petersburg grandees to tears, and I once heard Yevtushenko declaim a thrilling stream of Russian (he was a shameless ham). Hugo Williams wrote recently in the *Times Literary Supplement* that the poem is hardly the point; the punters are there to stare at these figures on stage, to see if they match up to preconceptions of the bard. But at Cambridge I too often found poets on stage depressing.

Just lately I have again begun to take pleasure in such occasions. Indeed, it would have been a dull soul who did not enjoy hearing the Australian (and Catholic) Les Murray in St Andrews, describing that town as a Reformation bomb site.

At the opening of the Cambridge Poetry Festival, all those decades ago, the coordinator Richard Burns gave a speech of welcome at which he claimed that such gatherings are essential in order to bring practitioners together, because otherwise writing poetry is such a lonely art. As a writer in a garden hut myself, I do sympathise, but I know why many prefer to keep the reading of poetry a similarly lonely activity.

12. FELONS

Over the years I've had a few encounters with crime and the law, and if nothing else I've learned how very variable is the status of truth.

When I was fourteen my school took us camping for a week. One activity was a day's walk across Dartmoor, and I set off with my pal Tom. The day was hot; we came upon a pub by a river and, to our delight, they readily sold us a lot of Guinness. On we wobbled, until we encountered the only roadworks in the middle of Dartmoor. We thought one of those red oil lanterns would look splendid outside our tent, so we picked it up and staggered forward, only to meet the one police Land Rover in the middle of Dartmoor.

We were let off with cautions, thoroughly alarmed. Before being released we were interviewed separately, Tom first in the Land Rover; these days we'd have thrown a snappy counter-charge of molestation. When it was my turn Tom muttered, 'Stick to your story.' I thought: I haven't got a story. So I told the truth, but was now terribly concerned that it was not enough. I longed to embroider. In this instance, truth did not seem nearly adequate.

Two years later, I went to stay with friends in Strasbourg, returning via an overnight train to Dunkirk. There were few other passengers: in our compartment, just myself and a youngish French businessman. There was space for each of us to lie down along the seats and sleep, and my companion hung his jacket by the window. I lay in a state of semi-slumbering half-consciousness. At some point in the night, I was vaguely aware that the train had stopped, and another man entered the compartment. He sat quietly as we moved off. After a few minutes he stood up. I saw him move to the window, go back to the door, and leave. In the morning, the businessman's wallet had gone, with several hundred francs.

Of course, he suspected me. I didn't know what to say; I could hardly tell him that I had watched his wallet being stolen. In this instance, the truth was unspeakable.

In my year off before university, I was a Community Service Volunteer in the north of England working at a 'family advice centre' on a grim housing estate. One day a friendly hooligan called Billy took my motorbike and set off for a spin around the estate, straight into the arms of the law. Social Services now had a problem: Billy had a long record and, if he were prosecuted, would be straight back to borstal. So they asked me (aged 18) if I would take the rap, saying that I'd let Billy borrow the bike. The deal was, Social Services paid any fines: naively, I agreed. They found me an excellent lawyer, a very senior figure in the local Labour Party. What no one pointed out was the record and license endorsement I would receive. In this instance, the truth was decidedly inconvenient.

As an undergraduate, that motorbike got me into more trouble: I was apprehended for riding ten feet across the pavement, nipping between one-way systems. I decided to go to court, purely out of curiosity. My own case was of no interest, but the case preceding was memorable. A man had been stopped for speeding in his car. He had turned out of a side-road, driven a short distance on the main road, then turned off again. It so happened that a police motorcyclist was behind him and declared him to be doing fifty.

The driver conducted his own spirited defence. He'd obtained the manufacturer's acceleration figures for the car. He'd gone out and measured the length of main road he'd covered. He demonstrated in

172

court that it was mechanically and mathematically impossible for his car to have reached the speed he was accused of.

But the lady magistrate had just one question:

'A Rover 2000, that's a fast car, isn't it?'

– before pronouncing him guilty. I remember the incredulity on the driver's face as he blurted out: 'Guilty?!' In this instance, the truth was disregarded.

Walking through London soon after, I saw a taxi knock a motorcyclist off his bike. As an outraged fellow biker, I hurried over and offered my (unhurt) compadre my phone number as a witness.

'But what did you witness?' protested the cabby.

'I saw you knock him off!' I retorted, then stopped short. No, I hadn't seen that. I'd heard a crash, seen a biker on the ground and a taxi swerving. That's all. Had the cabby not challenged me, I'd have sworn he hit the biker. I now wanted to ask for my phone number back. In this instance, the truth was... well, I don't know what it was, but I might have gone to court for it.

13. LIBRETTO

To the opera: a 'traditional' production of *Carmen*, sung by Moldovans and Ukrainians and including gypsy dancers and a real horse! A peerless white Andalucian stallion there on stage, the very beast that featured in the film *Gladiator*. Fabulous! Except that, because we saw the show in Dundee instead of Edinburgh, we didn't get the horse. It was in the small print at the bottom of the poster: Dundee – no horse.

For Moldovans, their National Opera (said the programme) is a major currency earning export, winning the gratitude of the nation. Worldwide, music-drama has startlingly varied significance. Many countries now see it as a way of re-packaging local lore for the modern world. As a VSO in Indonesia in the 1970s, I found that a state-sponsored 'new opera' had been created using puppets and the music of the gamelan. The local musicians and perhaps the tourists were suspicious of something so synthetic, and it petered out. I once visited Nicaragua and bought the entire catalogue of Sandinista music, two dozen or so recordings. These included the *Canto Epico del FSLN* ('Epic Song of the Sandinista Front'), the revolution retold in song. I've still got it; it's rather good, vigorous and tuneful.

My own stage singing career began when Edinburgh Grand Opera produced Britten's *Peter Grimes* at the Festival Theatre, and I learned what it was like to walk onto a huge stage and sing your heart out in a massive, complex drama, with fifty other wildly excited amateurs. Heaven knows what it sounded like, but it was one of the most thrilling things I've ever done. I am now looking for funds with which to write an opera of my own. Like heroin, it's an addictive and costly business.

174

Musicians sometimes assert that the music is all that counts, but they're demonstrably wrong. Successful operas have powerful and involving stories, even if they're overblown, rhetorical, indeed operatic. Poor storylines lose their audience early in the second act. As a dramatist, I've devised several tales as the basis for libretti. All I need now is a composer and a great deal of money.

My first attempt at a libretto concerned a Latino revolution and a competition for propaganda songwriters: a Sandinista *Meistersinger*. A friendly director wanted to stage it in a multi-story car park in Edinburgh; inexplicably, the Scottish Arts Council balked.

A composer once called me, proposing to enter a competition in London; it seemed a splendid opportunity. He, however, wanted to determine the subject, which illustrates my dictum above. His scenario was Rudolph Hess flying to Scotland, while British politicians debated the niceties of dealing with a Nazi. He envisaged Hess singing everything from the cockpit, while the likes of Chips Channon pondered him from below. I couldn't see it. When he said that the story didn't matter anyway, that it was only a peg for music, I knew we wouldn't get along.

A more sympathetic Scottish composer considered one of my own storylines, but what could we do without money? I am economical with my material (and why not? Henry James's *Turn of the Screw* exists as a short story, a stage play and an opera). So I sadly recycled my redundant libretto as a short story.

A delightful project came up: a musical for a consortium of primary schools. It was Millennium Year, and for once there were funds available. What would be the subject? It was the year of the Devolution Referendum, and I thought of re-working *Passport to Pimlico* with a Highland town suddenly discovered to be independent according to a medieval treaty. It could have been funny, and it seemed the ideal moment for children to explore issues of responsibility, and what it meant to take power on your own account, like the Sandinistas. But word came back that the funding authorities wouldn't touch this: it would apparently have been seen as propaganda for the SNP.

We opted for the notion of a town girl taking a dream journey downriver, and we listed the scenes: markets, a ruined castle, a fair, and that centrepiece of any decent Highland stream, a distillery. But again, objections: we shouldn't promote spirits in primary schools. The scene was cut – until influential figures intervened: the Region was famous for its distilleries, its economic heart was in its distilleries. Sing the Distilleries! It was back in, but as a musical interlude without words.

Bit by bit we worked it out, and Ronald McDonald paid for the children to fly down to London, stay three days and perform our show at the Millennium Dome. I'm uncertain whether the Millennium Dome is a smart venue to have on one's CV, but I see it as a stepping stone to *Ensign Ewart*, my fully-horsed spectacular, soon to be lavishly mounted at Covent Garden.

14. WHITE CHOCOLATE

My first play was produced in London in 1982, and the Bush Theatre issued a flyer describing me (correctly) as 'Jamaican-born'. A well-known listings magazine sent someone to interview me. When we were introduced, this person blinked at me in confusion because I am white and have an English public school voice – so where was the Jamaican-born playwright? The penny dropped at last; the interview was curt and cross, and was never published.

The more people pigeon-hole me, the more I struggle. Application forms for posts in the NHS ask that I specify my ethnic origins; in order to needle the statisticians, I put 'white Caribbean'. As an English writer living in Scotland, I am often re-labelled. In the USA I am reviewed as a 'Scottish playwright', while an Aberdeenshire newspaper once called me 'the quintessential wandering Scot'. At last year's Edinburgh Book Festival, I much appreciated the offer of a reading slot, but I had the choice of appearing either as a 'New Scottish Voice' (never mind I'd been writing professionally for twenty years) or as a 'Celtic Writer for Breakfast'. I opted for the latter: one got a croissant, at least.

Writers working abroad come up against objections if they express opinion about the locals, or put words into local mouths. I have been given to understand, by an actress rehearsing a play of mine in Edinburgh, that I had no right to present a particular view of Scottish culture because I'm no Scot.

Perhaps I should claim that I am. The Macallan/SoS story competition is open to anyone 'Scottish by association', a cunning formula. I knew a family in Aberdeen whose children grew up considering themselves to be Scots, and to meet the family you'd have agreed. In fact both the mother's parents were English; she just happened to be born near Edinburgh. Her husband, meanwhile, was of London-Austrian-Jewish stock who had come to Scotland as a student. But both had the manner, the accent, even a taste for Tennents lager. They'd adopted an identity.

One can always set up shop on one's own. In the mid-80s I worked in Burma with the Karen, an ethnic group who have been fighting for their independence since 1948. The Karen long ago despaired of any justice from the Burmese, and declared themselves autonomous. They created a rainforest state called Kawthoolay, or 'Flowerland'. This state had its own laws, an army, Government Departments of Education and Health, all run from huts in the forest. What it did not have was recognition from anyone else, except a few other rebels in Burma. As far as the outside world was concerned, Kawthoolay did not exist, yet the Karen living there considered themselves to be its citizens.

We are, very largely, whoever we declare that we are, especially in Britain where it is quite legal to go under any name one chooses. My small claim to Scottishness comes through my mother: she had Shetland grandparents, Sandersons of Lerwick. But many Shetlanders do not see themselves as Scots. I could claim Norwegian descent.

On my father's side, the 'dominant' strain came from Guernsey with a French Huguenot (Calvinist) ancestry. Some people with this background consider themselves somehow French or 'Huguenot'. I had a schoolfriend whose family traced their descent and their identity even further back to the English King Henry II (died 1189). For them, there was meaning in the claim, a heritage, but mathematically it is ridiculous. There is a simple way to illustrate this.

178

Assume four generations per century: Henry II died 814 years ago, giving us 32 generations. On your calculator, multiply 2x2x2x... thirty-two times: this will give you the number of ancestors you had at the time of the king's death. But you will never achieve the result on a domestic calculator, because the total – very many millions – will be way off the scale. Potentially, any of those millions contributed to your genetic make-up.

My earliest Guernsey ancestor whose name I know was born *c*.1780. At that short range, I have some 500 forebears. I, however, draw a narrow thread on the family tree, linked by a name. I surely have African, Chinese, Arab, Jewish and any amount of other 'blood', but by convention I identify only my patrilineal family and the Huguenots, of whom I'm proud.

We are, I believe, all of us racially prejudiced, insofar as we identify with certain groups and distinguish ourselves from others about whom we hold opinions. I am particularly prejudiced as regards the Spanish, the Dutch and the Chinese: I like them, for no particular reason, and if I am introduced to one I make a pre-judgement in their favour. If I researched long enough, I could probably find a Chinese and a Dutch ancestor, way back; perhaps I could adopt their name and identify with them. I could bring up my little son as a Sino-Hollander.

Unless, of course, he chooses to call himself a Norwegian.

15. CONSHIES

In 1990 I spent Christmas in an iced-up farmhouse in France. As we drove home, on the opposite carriageway of the autoroute a stream of trucks in desert camouflage headed south.

'The French setting off to war,' said my sister.

Returning to Aberdeenshire, I found that someone had convened an evening gathering for neighbours to talk about how they felt about the inevitable Gulf War that was coming. Soon after, our various families met in the pub. There were children there, including a teenage girl called Becky. As we talked I realised that the adults' remarks were largely directed towards her. We were keen for Becky to know that, although our generation could do nothing to stop the fighting, we did not approve. We wanted her to remember that.

I wanted no part of this war on Iraq. When my little boy Kit grows up, he may enquire about what his parents thought and did, and I cannot bear the idea that he might think I approved.

This lily-livered streak in me goes way back. One fondly imagines that one reaches opinions by personal ratiocination, but of course many opinions one simply inherits. While one of my grandfathers was an artilleryman who survived the Great War from end to end, the other was a lawyer MP who in 1915 risked his career by defending and sheltering conscientious objectors, Lytton Strachey among them. In WWII my father flew in Swordfish biplanes defending Arctic conveys – as perilous a posting as one could find – but my mother spent her time in the company of 'conshies' working as porters in a hospital. I started young, joining the first Aldermaston March into Tralalgar Square. I was five, I believe, and my photo

180

appeared in the Daily Telegraph carrying a huge CND placard and escorted by an Old English sheepdog called Snowball. To this day I make a monthly payment to CND.

In the 1980s I trained as nurse in Oxford, and joined two other organisations. One was the Peace Tax Campaign, a Quaker group who argued 'for the legal right of redirection of taxes from military to peace-building purposes, on grounds of conscience.' I edited the local newsletter, taking as inspiration Henry Thoreau's fine essay, *On Civil Disobedience* (1848). Thoreau objected to forced contributions to the Church, to slavery, to war, and was concerned about the implications of passive acquiescence in what Government does in our name:

> Voting is a sort of gaming with a moral tinge. The character of the voters is not staked. I cast my vote... but am not vitally concerned that the right prevail. I am willing to leave it to the majority... Voting for the right is doing nothing for it... is only expressing feebly your desire that right should prevail.

The other organisation was the Medical Campaign Against Nuclear Weapons. I wore their enamelled badge on my nursing uniform, expecting some irate Nursing Officer to order me to remove it and wondering whether I would stand my ground. That point never came. Then the local CND (which included several of my nursing clique) organised a blockade of the US Air force base at Upper Heyford. As a blockade it was hardly impressive: Thames Valley Police were there in greater numbers than us, effectively blockading the base themselves. We would march over the road and sit down, only to be hauled away. We achieved one good laugh. Our group was code-named 'Graham' and we would call to each other by that name. We soon noted senior police officers instructing their men that at all costs the ringleader Graham should be identified and arrested.

What saddened me was the reaction of my profession. I was advised by my nursing tutors that I was very fortunate not to have been arrested myself, as I could have been disciplined for bringing the profession into disrepute. Disrepute? Nurses, protesting against conflict? They should have been proud of us; at least we tried. An attempt by the Royal College of Nursing to organise a conference on The Medical Implications of Nuclear War collapsed through apathy.

I once attempted to force my Oxfordshire Parish Council to debate the Government's instruction that they draw up emergency plans for nuclear conflict. I failed: it transpired that my house was the wrong side of the parish boundary. At least in Fife I have my little boy well away from Upper Heyford. Unfortunately we now have to fear Saddam's Scuds directed against Leuchers. Where should I take Kit? Is Cape Wrath safe?

Just before the outbreak of World War II, a certain American dignitary told his friends that the world was becoming altogether too tense and risky – the Continental US at any rate – and as a sensible man he was removing himself from harm's way. He had, he said, chosen his place of refuge, a small, peaceful island basking in the sun miles from anywhere. The oncoming conflict should not find him. The name of this island? Guam.

16. ASYLUM

We are to receive dispersed asylum seekers in Fife and, for my part, they are most welcome. We Fallas have a tradition of succouring asylum seekers. My ancestor, Captain Falla of Les Camps, Guernsey, gave his daughter Kate in marriage to one James Le Page whose family were Huguenots, refugees from French religious intolerance. They were seafarers; great-great-grandfather Captain Pierre was drowned on his first voyage after his marriage. Today, my sister and my niece live in Spitalfields, London, in houses that were built by Huguenot silk workers. Each house has a large, open plan top floor, where the spinning was done.

After the Huguenots, Spitalfields received a wave of Jews. Soon Hawksmoor's masterpiece, Christ Church, was only yards away from a synagogue, and the fur traders and bagel bakers were setting up shop in Brick Lane. After the Jews came the Bengalis, and today one of the churches has become a mosque. Bagels now rub shoulders with birianis.

Asylum seekers and illegal immigrants enrich our lives, and I have tried to do my bit on their behalf. Some twenty years ago I continued the family tradition by volunteering to marry one. I was a student nurse in Oxford, she was an Iranian fleeing the Ayatollahs, and I thought it a fine and romantic way to strike a blow for liberty. When we were introduced, she appeared less impressed. Over tea in my damp basement kitchen, she seemed a hard, calculating woman. She had been wealthy in Iran, and possibly found a marriage of convenience to a penniless student nurse unappealing. I never heard from her again.

On behalf of our village hall, I lately completed a Lottery application. The form specifically asked whether our project would benefit asylum seekers or refugees. How sad, to answer 'no'.

I have persevered. I've tried to interest film and TV companies in romantic thrillers based around asylum seekers. One script was called *The Rose Girl,* and centred on young women who stand at traffic lights or motorway off-ramps selling flowers to commuters. I imagined a wealthy businessman falling in love with such a girl and being drawn into the desperate politics of her people, be they Hispanics in Los Angeles or Gulf Arabs in London.

At that time, I had a Fulbright Fellowship at a Los Angeles film school. The students were rich kids who came to classes in Jeeps and Mustangs. My wife meanwhile was a volunteer at the Clinica Oscar Romero; her clientele were Salvadoreans fleeing civil war, who didn't dare go to the city hospitals for fear of being reported to Immigration. Having had no antenatal care whatever, they would come in off the street unannounced and go into labour in the little clinic's foyer.

But in neither LA nor the UK could I arouse enthusiasm for my film ideas. There would be no audience, Hollywood executives told me; whites would rather not think about the ill-paid drudges on whom their lifestyles depended, while Hispanics wanted only to forget, wanted only to watch Seinfeld or Schwarzenegger – so the producers averred. Back in Britain, I was hired by the producers of the TV series *Bliss* (about a Cambridge scientist investigating skulduggeries), but when I came up with a story focused on asylum seekers, I was dropped.

I have lately completed a film script called *Jacky Whisky* concerning the Poles who reached Scotland in the 1940s. Like my Huguenot

184

forebears three centuries before, the Poles were initially welcome. But the tone of the war changed; we were allies with Stalin who wanted Poland, so these un-communist refugees were labelled as untrustworthy, though they (and the Czechs) had outflown everybody in the Battle of Britain. By 1944, Poles were being beaten up on Clydeside by union men who said they threatened Scottish jobs. My script awaits its maker.

A few such films have succeeded. Ken Loach made *Bread and Roses*, based on scriptwriter Paul Laverty's encounters with Hispanic janitors in Los Angeles. *Beautiful People*, concerning Bosnian Serbs and Muslims in London, was one of the most life-enhancing films made in the UK for decades.

Gregory Nava's *El Norte* depicted Guatemalans entering the USA by crawling through a rat-infested tunnel. The analogy is apt, and my own solution to the problem of illegal immigration is simple: we must encourage it. Anyone who looks dispassionately at the demography of Western Europe sees that, with our populations ageing and shrinking (numerically and mentally), we badly need immigrants to revive both our workforce and our culture. Populists cannot bear this truth, and I have never heard a politician with the balls to admit that we should abolish immigration controls entirely, though we in Fife are desperate for young blood. A new Channel Tunnel should be dug, surfacing at Burntisland; anyone with the nerve to stow away on a train to Burntisland must qualify for citizenship. We need all the help we can get. I am, however, no longer able to offer my hand in marriage.

17. XANADU

We all have certain books that haunt us. One of mine is a work of scholarship by an American, John Livingstone Lowes, published in 1927 and called *The Road to Xanadu*. I first read it in my teens, and have returned to the book and its ideas repeatedly since.

The Road to Xanadu is subtitled 'a study in the ways of the imagination.' It concerns Coleridge and the processes by which he wrote *Kubla Khan* and *The Rime of the Ancient Mariner*, and it explores the poems by a very particular means, picking apart every line, every phrase word by word to establish Coleridge's sources. It is an extraordinary feat of close enquiry into anything and everything Lowes believed Coleridge to have read, volume after volume scrutinised in minute detail. So, for instance, convinced that Coleridge had seen the 1772 *Opticks* of Joseph Priestley, Lowes read it too — all 807 pages of it — to see if he could spot any proof that Coleridge had drawn on it for his poems. For 806 pages, Lowes drew a blank, but on page 807 there is an assertion that if two candle flames are held close together, the light given out is greater than two candles separately. And Coleridge in a notebook had stored this away, calling it a 'picture of Hymen.'

Line by line, Lowes rummages through Coleridge's vast reading, finding scores of fragments tucked deep in the creative mind, or in (as Lowes calls it) 'that heaving and phosphorescent sea below the verge of consciousness'. As well as science, Coleridge devoured traveller's journals and histories, and for the *Ancient Mariner* dug out an old story that in 1668 a crescent moon was seen with a star within the two horns. Somewhere in the poet's psyche, other fragments came together telling how both ships and fish in certain 'rotting' and 'slimy' seas give off streams of shining phospher as they move.

186

What is this creative process, asks Lowes? He borrows a phrase from Henry James, and calls it 'the Well'. The dark waters of that well teem with everything the writer has ever read or ever seen, and down there things gel, fuse and combine using 'the hooks and eyes of memory' (Coleridge's phrase). Then, without warning, the new compounds surface as art.

Why the fascination for me? I know for certain that I am not a genius. But I also know that I am a real writer, and once I'd read *The Road to Xanadu* I couldn't help but detect a similar process in my own work. I revise my prose obsessively, and as I speak each sentence aloud, I often realise that I am using a turn of phrase or a tiny detail whose source I can locate in my memory, often items that have no seeming relation to what I'm now writing.

So, on the first page of my first novel *Blue Poppies,* I describe a Tibetan tax officer who 'rode about on business with his nose in the air,' not because I have any personal experience of Tibetan revenue men, but because I have in my 'well' the equestrian statue of Colleoni in Venice which I'd blended with Goya's Duke of Wellington and the hooded eyes and hooked snout of Piero's portrait of the Duke of Urbino. Later in the same novel, there's a coarse exchange in the Tibetan village about the smell of market women. 'Been sniffing up close, have you?' squawks a harridan – and buried in my mind is a report I once saw of an experiment into women's sense of smell, including a photograph of a line of men with one arm raised and a woman sniffing each oxter. Just over the page in my novel, the lead Tibetan woman watches from a window as the Scottish lead male rides towards her up a lane, and this scene is lifted wholesale from Chaucer's *Troilus*. When, a few pages later, 'At the end of March, flights of geese were seen,' that's from something Russian, but I can't remember what. I know it's there in my 'well', though. I can almost feel its presence, physically. On the following page, there's mention of Chinese soldiers fleeing in 1950 to join the Kuomintang in exile in Siam – and I met those Kuomintang, now very elderly, in a backwater of Thailand in 1987.

It can be less specific, just a turn of phrase or a pattern of speech not my own but recalled from my father, or from a friend, or a chance conversation. In William Nicholson's 1990 television play *The March* there's an exchange out in the desert between a hungry African and a European aid worker on the subject of cats. I remember it as follows:

> African: They give more food to cats.
>
> European woman: Cats?
>
> African: That's a small furry animal…
>
> European: Yes, I know what a cat is!

In my *Blue Poppies,* this reappears with the Tibetan woman telling the Scottish character that her dead husband has been reincarnated as a yak.

> 'A yak?' queried Jamie.
>
> 'It is the big animal with much hair…'
>
> 'Oh, yes, I know.'

I have a notion that, in my final decline, I will spend some months annotating a copy of each of my books to point up these sources, echoes and borrowings. I'll present these copies to the British Library, to illustrate 'the hooks and eyes of memory' at work in the creative process. What a pathetic, vain project, who could possibly be interested!

Well, John Livingstone Lowes would have been, as might Coleridge.

WHAT YOU SEEK IS WHAT YOU'LL GET

1. AMONG MUSLIMS

In November 2001, a dozen Pakistani men (actually from Pakistan) walked into Newburgh, our little town in Fife, sat down on the pavement and began reading aloud from the Qur'an. It was a four-month Peace Walk, Aberdeen to Glasgow, to promote mutual understanding. They'd set off before September 11th. The first local to approach them was our poet Kathleen Jamie, out shopping with her children, who ten years previously had made a journey to Pakistan that had coloured her thinking profoundly. She'd written a book about it, *The Golden Peak*.

But now Newburgh's good Christian folk declined to accommodate wandering Muslims; overnight accommodation at the church hall was refused. Quietly outraged, Jamie recalled a complete stranger in Pakistan hastening to help her, declaring that he must of course assist because 'it is my honour'. So Jamie and her husband now scurried about Newburgh because 'it is my honour' and they found the Peace Walkers an empty shop in which to camp. Oddly, the very next day, a publisher rang to ask about her ten-year-old book, and whether she'd be interested in a return to Pakistan.

So there appeared *Among Muslims*, the original text plus a new prologue and epilogue, and a better emissary from Scotland to the Karakoram could hardly be imagined. In her poetry, Jamie has shown sensitivity to the presence of Muslims in Scotland, a presence not greatly valued otherwise. For Pakistan – landscape and people – she displays a deep warmth unencumbered by illusion.

189

Wandering in mountain towns and villages, she resolves to see clearly, and does see babies 'plentiful, plump and ghastly with kohl smudged round their staring eyes' and a friend wearing a shalwa kameez in turquoise rayon and a leopard-spot print. This particular family – Rashida, and her mother and sisters – are Shia girls whose purdahed life Jamie cannot fully share, which yet seems to offer a tranquillity, a quality of 'lightness' that at last she finds almost irritating. They in turn are intrigued by Jamie, her lack of a husband, her 'not beautiful' shoes. They'd love her to stay, to marry, to understand.

Their old mother's lifestyle, she realises, is not dissimilar from that of her own Renfrewshire grandmother: constrained, limited, fond of gardens, humane. Some of the younger women are startlingly well educated. They may not know where Fife is, but when a woman addresses Jamie, we discover that English is this person's *seventh* language. Does anyone in Scotland speak seven languages – apart, perhaps, from some of our Pakistanis?

This female slant is balanced by sharp but sympathetic portraits of men; the splendid retired Major, booming his outspoken politics; the flagellants at the Mutharam ceremony, whipping themselves with razor blades, who lash harder because a white woman is watching; the quiet scholar, compiling a history of Baltistan. She hears the Ismaili people called I-smiley, and cannot but agree.

What of her return, a decade later? The Shia girls were still there, somewhat worn down with family responsibility. The reunion was happy, but not overly joyous. The Major was now a politician. The referendum-rigging General Musharraf was, seemingly, popular. But a melancholy had overtaken everything.

190

When I visited Pakistan in the mid-seventies, the country was said to be controlled by the 'Three Ms' – the Military, the Mullahs, and the aMericans. On her first trip, Kathleen Jamie had felt it to be a land of hope, where people believed in their country and its future, however poor they might be. But now the world was crowding in. Since Alexander the Great, the country has never been short of tourists or visiting generals. Now it had refugees and Taliban too.

Book reviewing gives one a curious view of contemporary preoccupations. I was once sent a volume of essays discussing the state of the world from the point of view of Médecins Sans Frontières; MSF were quite clear that the cause of most trouble was still Communism. That was in 1998, and that fixation would change. After 9:11, I began reviewing more regularly for *Scotland on Sunday*, receiving books which addressed Islam from differing viewpoints in almost all of which it was associated with violence. Kathleen Jamie's subtle, empathetic, open-hearted view of Muslim society was not what usually arrived. How rare it was to have any normality or decency portrayed. Oddly enough, all the other books were by men.

I had lived for two years in Indonesia, in Bandung, a big, crowded industrial-cum-university city. Islam was all around me, a peaceable set of values by which my pleasant and friendly neighbours and colleagues lived. How strange, years later, to contemplate the fanatical faith portrayed in book after book published in the UK. Most authors still regarded Islam as the 'other' whose violence must be explained, sometimes in savage histories that seemed hardly changed since the poems of Henry Newbolt or the Retreat from Kabul. It was unsurprising that after 9:11 writing on the 'threat' of Islam proliferated, but the writers fed prejudices even as they strove to 'understand'.

191

Jason Burke, the *Observer's* chief reporter, spent much of his career in Islamic countries almost synonymous with conflict, from Pakistan to Algeria, and starting with a hare-brained, hair-raising escapade as a volunteer peshmerga with an AK47 in Kurdistan, where he and a fellow student signed up for adventure. Realising that Burke and friend were of more value as propaganda than as cannon fodder, the Kurds made sure that everyone saw them and that they stayed out of trouble. When shooting started, Burke was usually lying flat in a ditch.

Two decades on, Burke was the author of a widely-read study of Al-Qaeda and other works on militant Islam. *On The Road to Kandahar* was a memoir of assignments to Muslim hot spots, chasing interviews with people who might or might not be close to Osama bin Laden, hanging out with US forces in Baghdad, and being shelled on arid mountainsides. As I read the review copy, a depressing sense of *déjà vu* set in. Journalists' travelogues from these dangerous regions were already becoming commonplace; Burke insisted that most Afghan civilians 'just wanted to get by and put dinner on the table', but those dinners were not described. One marvelled at his courage or lunacy at pursuing informants under fire; however, one alarming encounter with bearded men toting rocket grenades is pretty much like another.

Burke's travels were billed as an attempt to 'understand Islam, and Islamic radicalism.' There was little of the former; the religion itself was hardly discussed. Burke was, however, open to the experience of the footsoldiers. He declined to dismiss the Taliban as barbarians who imprison women, reminding us that the movement began with Mullah Omar incensed by the abduction and rape of a village girl, and his lynching of the perpetrator. The Taliban that Burke met were often young, naïve, poorly educated, and simplistic in their

192

world view, but they were not the psychopaths of popular belief, maddened by bloodlust and sodomy, the image fostered by Khaled Hosseini's bestselling novel *The Kite Runner*.

Burke concluded that violence to women, such as he saw almost unquestioned in Pakistan (a quite different view from that of Kathleen Jamie) often coincides with periods of rapid change in women's status; he might have recalled our own suffragettes, who were subjected to considerable physical violence. Many Islamist warriors that he met, far from being part of a global conspiracy, were simply locals who had banded together to resist humiliation at the hands of invaders. Burke was alert to history, demonstrating how Donald Rumsfeld's 2003 announcement that the Coalition had come to Iraq 'not to occupy but to liberate' was echoing the British entering Baghdad in 1919, who in turn echoed Napoleon capturing Alexandria in 1798.

But Burke's Islamic world was a limited one; no mention of Indonesia, by far the largest Muslim country. His perspective consisted of little but conflict, although his conclusion – that extremist violence alienates its own populations and must therefore wither away – was curiously hopeful.

Burke was the sort of writer drawn to the world's trouble spots – and any Islamic society was a trouble spot by definition. For the trauma surgeon and self-confessed disaster junkie Jonathan Kaplan (*Contact Wounds*, 2005) the main interest in Iraq was that appalling things happened there which required his specialist skills. He needed this, and used it as a sort of release: 'Every day I scan the war news like job-vacancy ads, searching for peace.' He yearned to be 'lost in this incomprehensible communion' of fellowship under fire.

The Middle East gave him that. He was least sufficiently clear-sighted to see the idiocy of the so-called 'aid agencies' who waited in Jordan poised to swoop in the wake of the Coalition invasion, groups with names like The Good People, Oasis of Love, and Human Appeal International, for whom an Islamic disaster was an open invitation to meddle.

Other books arriving for review made no attempt to dilute the horrors of Muslim society new or old. Giles Milton's *White Gold* (2004) told the story of Thomas Pellow, a young Cornish seaman captured and taken to Morocco as a slave in 1715, who later wrote an account of his misadventures; also of the psychopathic Sultan Moulay Ismail and the 'one million white slaves' languishing in North Africa. Milton's popular history played to the gallery, and he loved to set a colourful scene:

> Only the vizier, sweltering in his leopardskin pelt, dared to wipe the beads of sweat from his brow...

This was complete fiction, of course; one was being encouraged to let the imagination range freely, and Milton supplied a setting that allowed for those imaginings to be lurid, akin to paintings of white sex slaves for sale in the souks of Araby as painted by Gerome, or *The Death of Sardanapalus* by Delacroix. In fact, Thomas Pellow almost certainly exaggerated his own memoir to make it more saleable in London, but that didn't bother Milton who did little to disguise his prejudices; he seldom missed a chance to remind us that the villains were black – black slave drivers, black guards, black executioners.

The title of Fergus Fleming's *The Sword & the Cross* (2003) announced that here was another book placing Muslims in a context of violence, this time focussing on a 19th century French colonial army general and a priest who acted the hermit but who spied for the colonial power. In this story the French came off badly, a picture of brutality and incompetence. But again, the story could only view Muslim Africa in terms of conquest and resistance, and was predictably one-sided. Knowing no Arabic, Fleming had consulted no African sources for his history. So, when a French military expedition is annihilated in the sands, we learn of this via French reports only – a view no more rounded than, say, the *Illustrated London News* reporting the British destruction of Benin in 1897, with Africa reduced to an arena for violence and any encounter with Islam a matter for 'the sword'.

General Laperrine's last words, quoted by Fleming, were: 'People think they know the desert [but] nobody really knows it.' Europeans probably not – but one could try asking the people who live there.

Charles Allen, veteran historian of British India (where he was born), also offered to explain the dangers of Islam that we had supposedly taken our eyes off. Allen, like Jason Burke and Kathleen Jamie in their different ways, was at home on the turbulent Muslim frontiers, but Allen's view like Fleming's was historical. In *God's Terrorists* (2006) he explored the long confrontation between the Western Powers (represented by the soldier-sahibs of British India) and Wahhabi Islam which originated in 18th century Arabia; following earlier desert Arab puritans, Muhammad ibn Abd-al-Wahhab taught a creed that was reductionist, stripping the faith to fundamentals. This teaching flourished in the wild Afghan borderlands, inspiring the 'Hindustan Fanatics' in the cities of northern India to menace the British Raj, sending a steady flow of recruits to trouble the North West Frontier. Wahhabism crystallised the resentments that exploded in the Sepoy Mutiny of 1857. Later, as taught in the madrassah at Deoband near Delhi, it provided an ideological focus for Islamic resistance to western Imperialism up to the present day, and for the thinking of the Taliban in Afghanistan, and of Al-Qaeda.

Allen's tales of the misadventures of Victorian District Commissioners, cavalry colonels and their Pathan adversaries were entertaining, with splendid vignettes such as the warriors glimpsing their leader dressed in white in the mouth of a cave, who they then discover is a literal man of straw, stuffed.

Allen, though, could not explain the persistent appeal of Wahhabism, beyond noting that Indian Muslims felt threatened by Victorian Christian evangelicals. Wahhabism is easily characterised as intolerant and violent, but Islam is hardly the first religion to produce waves of puritanism. A faith stripped to fundamentals, face to face with God without intermediary priests, is neither necessarily 'fanatical' nor retrogressive; it may simply be clear about what it believes. Why did so many youths offer themselves to Wahhabism? Was it just (as Allen suggests) that they were poor, illiterate and easily preyed upon by crafty mullahs? This recalls the naïve young men interviewed by Jason Burke, but it also patronises people who understood only too clearly that they were oppressed and exploited by British India. Puritan cults appeal to the downtrodden because they offer hope – but, in popular publishing, Islam was portrayed as grounded in a violence for which the most charitable explanation was naïvete.

I picked up a copy of the *Daily Mail* not long ago in which on every second page some crime or social woe was attributed to Muslims. In August 2017, the *Daily Telegraph* reported that a little girl from a dysfunctional British Christian household had been placed by social workers for emergency foster care with a Muslim family, who had

196

encouraged her to learn a bit of Arabic. Worse: the Muslim mother wore a burka. Never mind the welcome, the warmth, the refuge the girl found; this placement was seen as a violation of a child's rights and culture, as though those rights had been honoured by her own kin. As for learning Arabic! The girl would surely be recruited for ISIS or spirited away to the souks of Araby as another sex slave.

It was all nonsense. If the little girl had been given sanctuary by a French-speaking family, would the *The Telegraph* have noticed – even if she'd been encouraged to learn a little French? But if we are fed a view of modern Muslims as bearded men with rocket grenades, or given a history of psychopathic sultans prowling the harem, public responses to anything Islamic will be predictably crass, and expectations will surely be fulfilled.

2. ALL NEWS OUT OF AFRICA IS BAD

A by-product of the old colonies kicking out their European rulers is a clutch of memoirs of change written by white survivors, children who grew up in circumstances it can be difficult to imagine. The memoirs are valuable not least for depicting realities of colonial life. I was born in Jamaica in 1954 four years before independence, I left there sailing for Britain on a banana boat, and I remember nothing beyond vague family myths of idyll which are doubtless untrue but which seem pleasantly fuzzy now; there's a photo of me in a paddling pool on the lawn of the Governor's house, aged zilch. Would I want to know the truth? What would I think of the island today, if I 'went back'? And what if my father had accepted a teaching job in Africa instead of the Caribbean? The news from Africa could be very bad indeed.

197

Several memoirs reached me for review, two by Englishwomen and both subtitled 'An African Childhood'. Both girls came of parents who had fled to the colonies from the small dreariness of post-WW2 Britain. Both young women ended up in the USA, one 'as a psychotherapist' and the other 'in Wyoming' – which itself speaks of escape and healing. For both, it had been several decades before they'd been able to write it out.

Carolyn Slaughter became a novelist, except that the novels fell silent for twelve years until she succeeded in writing her painful history, *Before the Knife* (2002). The nub of the story is spelled out early: at the age of six, Slaughter is raped by her father, and the family self-destructs thereafter. The father is a brute of a colonial policeman who, when not violating his child, enjoys casually smacking her in the mouth. There is a hint that the policeman's own mother was partly to blame for his state of mind. His wife, meanwhile, sinks into profound depression almost before they reach Africa, and the gentle charms of Swaziland cannot cheer her for long. When they move to the Bechuanaland Protectorate (later Botswana), things get much worse. Their new world – the Kalahari Desert – is starkly beautiful but perilous; the little girl fears polio and snakes, both of which are omnipresent. Not only Carolyn's mother is in trouble; neighbour women, trapped by encroaching sands in their sweltering, struggling farmsteads, sit at their pianos and go mad. Only the Afrikaners, admired for their here-to-stay resilience, seem to have stomach for the fight. Carolyn is a survivor against heavy odds.

This is a harsh picture that readers of early Doris Lessing will recognise. One can only admire Carolyn Slaughter's courage and self-control in exorcising horrendous demons and managing to write good descriptive prose into the bargain.

In *Don't Let's Go to the Dogs Tonight* (2002), Alexandra Fuller's world is less Lessing, more *Flame Trees of Thika* – but with a nastily farcical streak. A cast of perennially bankrupt, absurdly optimistic British colonists impulsively buy dud farms in impossible places. This time it is 1960-70s Rhodesia, with civil war in full swing after Ian Smith's UDI.

> Mum says, 'Don't come creeping into our room at night.'
>   They sleep with loaded guns beside them on the bedside rugs. She says, 'Don't startle us when we're sleeping.'
>   'Why not?'
>   'We might shoot you.'

Fuller's parents are oddly engaging but also appalling in their contempt for the blacks. The children echo their parents, and the whole family cheers whenever there's a bang from the minefields on the Mozambique border.

Fuller has a sharp eye for grim comedy, especially on the part of her hard-drinking mother who floors all-comers with gin and diatribes, when not on horseback charging down the squatters. The details are telling, for instance the civic flowerbeds planted to spell out 'Welcome to Umtali' from which rebel sympathisers persistently remove one flower-letter to make it read, 'We come to Umtali'. The irate whites have their garden boys re-plant the missing consonant, but overnight it always goes again.

This is a blend of dark farce and astonishing self-delusion. Fuller's family came to Rhodesia from Kenya, saying, 'We couldn't stay there after Mau Mau', and they then heedlessly re-play all the land-grabbing arrogance which provoked that earlier tragedy. As surely as the Kikuyu rose up in Kenya, so the Ndebele and Shona rise in Rhodesia, even as Mr and Mrs Fuller swear solemnly that they will give their lives 'to keep one country white'. For an explanation of Robert Mugabe's loathing of the British, look no further.

Both women escaped and neither, I think, has been back to look at Africa again. Given that their memories are so awful, what would they think if they saw the continent now, divested of white authority?

Paul Theroux was not born in Africa but was a Peace Corps Volunteer in Nyasaland shortly before it became independent Malawi in 1964, and – again, nearly four decades later – he wanted to see what had happened to the land he remembered. He begins *Dark Star Safari* (2002) with the words, 'All news out of Africa is bad.' When I first reviewed the book I objected that this was not true, and that a number of wars had ended: I now wince to see that I held up the Congo and Eritrea as examples of hope. Nothing daunted by bad news, Theroux embarked on a journey of astonishing arduousness. He risked his neck in speeding, overcrowded buses with bald tyres, he was shot at by bandits, was robbed and spat at, obliged to sleep in malarial flop-houses and insanitary trains, and to wait interminably. I found such travel stressful in my twenties. Theroux was pushing sixty.

His journey was not without great pleasures; some of the best passages in *Dark Star Safari* are, simply, the pleasures. One such was crossing Lake Victoria on an elderly steamer lovingly maintained and efficiently operated by a crew who welcomed him as a non-paying honoured guest. Theroux is happiest in the company of humble people in backwaters. In Mozambique he paddles with guides in a dug-out canoe down the Shire River, and muses:

> 'Borne onward by the muddy water, watched by fishermen and herons and the pods of hippos, protected by Karsten

and Wilson, I was the nearest thing on earth to Huckleberry Finn.'

Other settings bring out fine descriptive writing. Here, he lies in a stiffling tent in the desert:

> 'There came a trotting sound, not one animal but lots of tiny hooves, like a multitude of gazelle fawns, so soft in their approach they were less like hoofbeats than the sound of expelled breaths, pah-pah-pah. They advanced on me, then up and over my tent, tapping at the loose fabric. It was rain.'

Of the notable encounters, my favourite is with the Ethiopian Nebiy Makonnen who languished as a political prisoner for ten years. The only book he and his 35 cell-mates had between them was a battered copy of *Gone With The Wind*, and so Makonnen translated it, writing his version on three thousad sheets of cigarette foil. On his release, he tracked down all these scraps and published them, and this is the version that Ethiopians now read. *Dark Star Safari* contains many such delights.

But what of the present state of Africa? Theroux paints an appalling picture. All around he sees decay and corruption: financial, political, and spiritual. Every city is a mouldering dump (for Theroux the ironic exception is Mugabe's Harare), every library is empty of books (all stolen), every road is horrific, every official obstructive and venal. Frequently weary and depressed, Theroux becomes contemptuous and irritable – and decidedly irritating himself.

Inaccuracies mar much of his interpretation. Recalling his Peace Corps years, he says of Kenya that, even in 1963, 'I already felt that I was looking at a British Colony that had hardly changed in one hundred years.' He may have felt this, but back in 1863 Kenya did not exist. It was hardly explored, let alone colonised. The first British penetration inland was Joseph Thomson's surveying expedition of 1883 when the few settlers were mostly German. The region only became a British Protectorate in 1896 and a Crown Colony called Kenya in 1920. The colonial backwater frozen in time is a myth.

If a writer's grasp of fact is tenuous, his knowledge of colonialism so shaky, what faith should one put in his memories and reflections? Theroux scatters African history throughout his book; if only he had checked his research. Looking merely at the first Sudan chapter, we find these claims: General Gordon was killed in Omdurman (no: he died on the steps of the Governor's palace in Khartoum, as every schoolboy once knew); Kitchener was sent to avenge Gordon's death and the expulsion of the British (no: in 1885 Britain was not the occupying power; Gordon worked for the Egyptian government, and his troops were Egyptian); Kitchener's gunboats were freighted up to Sudan and assembled at Khartoum (hardly likely, since when the British did arrive in 1893 Khartoum was abandoned, derelict, at the Mahdists' mercy and anyway some 200 miles upriver from Kitchener's railhead at Atbara).

It's all simple stuff; the mistakes are lazy. Another lazy notion is the term 'medieval' applied to the lanes of Harrar in Ethiopia (which would have had nothing on the alleys and wynds of 18th century Edinburgh) and also repeatedly to African markets. He describes street entertainers in a Zanzibar market as 'the medieval touch' – like the ceilidh band at a Scottish farmer's market? – and he calls Khartoum souk 'medieval' which is true neither literally (Khartoum began life as an Egyptian army camp in 1821) nor figuratively except in the banal sense that markets no doubt operate now much as they did a thousand years ago. Such markets abound throughout the modern world. Theroux must have seen scores of them.

Theroux is free with his contempt. He despises fellow Nile cruise passengers who love snippets of anecdotal history – although that is exactly what he offers. He, however, is not a tourist but a 'traveller', and 'I always dined alone'. Mocking renditions of local pronunciations are patronising and cheap; Theroux makes all Egyptians say 'bibble' for 'people'. Given his lack of Arabic, he's lucky they spoke with him at all, and it hardly speaks of affection for the old continent. An especially defenceless target is V.S.Naipaul. Theroux's reputation took a self-inflicted knock from his treatment of Naipaul and their thirty-year 'friendship' to which he devoted his uncharitable memoir, *Sir Vidia's Shadow*. Naipaul haunts *Dark Star Safari* like Banquo's ghost, Theroux missing few chances to recall the Trinidadian 'ranting' with fear of Africa, his novels vitiated by his fear.

Theroux's fiercest drubbing he reserves for aid workers in their white Land Rovers. Two of them decline to give him lifts; soon they are all subject to his vengeful scorn. He refers to them by the snide term 'agents of virtue' and he writes, 'They were in general oafish self-dramatizing prigs and often complete bastards.' Actually, the few he talks to are a couple of naïve but personally inoffensive English nurses, an heroic mine clearing specialist, and a bunch of ex-servicemen who have built the only river barge capable of carrying vehicles on the Lower Zambezi.

But if there is a thesis driving *Dark Star Safari*, it is that aid is largely responsible for Africa's woes. His evidence for this is curiously second-hand, from other people's books; in all his journey he visits not one such project. One might demur that wars and greed don't help, though he is surely right that Africa cannot recover until it is left to make decisions for itself. Theroux's scorn may verge on the hysterical, but one cannot deny him his anger, or his sadness. He revisits the school in Malawi where he once taught, forty years before. Then a proud and hopeful place, it is now virtually derelict.

Dark Star Safari is long, sometimes repetitive and often exasperating. It can also be beautiful, funny, perceptive and courageous. But Theroux's starting point seems to have been contempt, an attitude that appears in neither of the women's memoirs: horror, but not contempt. They were perhaps themselves too deeply embedded in the colonies to feel contempt, which is a more superficial response. Theroux found just what he expected to find; the news from Africa will always be bad, and what you seek is what you'll get.

MEDDLING IN DARFUR
Writing *Poor Mercy*

In 1982 I had a play produced at the Bush Theatre in London. It was called *Topokana Martyrs Day* and concerned the misadventures of a quartet of field staff at a remote African outpost of a British aid agency. The play did well – five productions in the UK and USA – and in one respect it is, I think, unique: I know of no other successful comedy about famine relief in Africa.

The comedy derived directly from my own experience. In 1981 I had worked for Oxfam as a junior field officer in Karamoja, eastern Uganda. The famine was real enough but, when I came home, I re-read my diaries and realised that they were pure farce. So I dramatised them. The satire was broad: one character, for instance, was named Mrs McAllister, the Commissioner for Disaster Coordination.

> *Ibis*: Is she any good at that?
> *Apoo*: Mrs McAllister, my sweet, has coordinated so many disasters so successfully that we are now blessed with the spectacle of uninterrupted catastrophe across three continents.

In 1991, ten years later almost to the day, I was in Darfur, Sudan, as Medical Programme Coordinator for an aid agency striving to prevent a threatened famine. This time, the comedy seemed to have gone out of the job; indeed, it was one of the most humiliating experiences of my working life. With a handful of nurses, two doctors and a few Land Rovers, we attempted to shore up local health systems while the major international donors were signally failing to supply meaningful quantities of food to the villages. The vastly expensive operation was, on the whole, a miserable failure.

It became clear that the government of Sudan was being wilfully obstructive, and that all the bluster of Washington, Brussels and Rome could do little about this. Meanwhile, the tribes were in violent ferment, rebellion was in the air and the Army was cheerfully making matters worse. This, remember, was in 1991; it was a situation in many respects repeated in 2004-5.

Home again, I felt that I must write about this, as I had about Uganda a decade before. This time, however, I felt no urge to broad satire. I wondered, what format should the piece now take? I attempted non-fiction, a collection of short stories, a film treatment… but none seemed to answer the magnitude of the subject. After much hesitation I settled on a novel, believing that only panoramic fiction would do.

There was no shortage of vivid material, and many of the episodes in the book are factual: the assault on the township of Wadaa, destroyed with incendiary rockets; the distribution of date-expired drugs and poisonous seed-corn; the ten-wheel truck found abandoned in the desert with blood splashed down its side – these are taken straight from my Darfur diaries, and are not funny.

On the other hand, grim humour has a way of resurfacing everywhere; I think this was Shakespeare's view: that there is no human situation so dire that it is does not contain elements of comedy. In my diaries I find a ceilidh, for instance, organised by aid staff, at which Sudanese male-only couples danced the Gay Gordons dressed in long white robes (they thought it hilarious). And there was the following sequence of radio messages, received over the course of one morning by our office in Darfur:

09.40 hrs: Expect delivery 10,000 tons high energy biscuits for children's supplementary feeding.
10.20 hrs: Correction: expect delivery 10,000 tins of high energy biscuits.
11.25 hrs: Correction: expect 10,000 biscuits.

We never got the biscuits. These messages are quite genuine and this, only slightly reworded, is how they appear in the novel.

An abundance of good material, however, does not of itself make for good fiction. One also requires a clear narrative, an organising principle and, above all, a calm state of mind that can perceive the universal behind the particular. For several years I struggled with the project, trying to achieve objective distance on the experience. Finally it was matter of time, and of removing myself from the story; so there is no Jonathan Falla character in the book.

The male lead of my novel *Poor Mercy* is an African, specifically a southern Sudanese, washed up by violence in the south and arriving in Darfur. His name is Mr Mogga; he's cherubic but ludicrous, shrewd but innocent, highly efficient but finally helpless. Like the hero of Conrad's *Nostromo*, he is the essential factotum without whom things fall apart. The foreigners come to rely on him entirely, while not noticing his growing doubts and fears. They take him for granted but fail to fully appreciate the extent of the peril that he is in, until very late in the day.

Mogga exemplifies a character type met frequently in aid work: the effective local staff-member, intelligent, adept at coping with a crisis, semi-educated by inadequate schools and semi-westernised in a sometimes destructive way, such that they are readily seduced and confused by foreign can-do attitudes, and by foreigners' seeming freedom to roam the world. These local people are terribly vulnerable. Employed by an aid agency as factotum and interpreter, such a person is responsible for conveying to their compatriots all the hope and grand promises that the agencies embody. When the promises fall flat and the schemes fail – as is so often the case – then the foreigners depart, and people like Mr Mogga are left to bear the brunt of the lingering resentment.

> 'Where's Mogga?' asked Rose 'What of him? What'll he do?'
> 'Well,' said Xavier, 'that's up to Mogga. He's a free man.'
> 'No,' exclaimed Rose Price, 'Mogga's not free at all, he's trapped here. With us gone, they'll be gunning for him.'
> Xavier looked more and more uncomfortable.
> 'He's not responsible for anything.'
> 'But they'll hold him responsible! They'll go for him; God knows what they'll do. If we run off, he'll be all that's left.'

Mogga is the go-between, the saviour of many situations – and the victim. He is, however, very astute. He is also the focus both of humour and of love, and his tender relationship with the sophisticated Arab scientist Leila forms the emotional heart of the story.

Theirs, too, is the wonder at an extraordinary, harshly beautiful landscape:

> Mid-afternoon, they were scudding over naka, hard soil that glittered with silicates. Then came black shale and pockets of ironflake where the desert was rusted. They continued due north, climbing steadily into starker lands. Now the crust was replaced by countless pebbles rolled against their neighbours until smooth and oval. The pebbles were spaced and spread evenly as far as the eye could see, like a grainy photo. In all that empty space, you could not lie comfortably down to

sleep; there would be no rest. Next there was lava detritus, and packed gravel. Furrows in the ground showed where once it had rained, but now the Land Rover was burning up, the dust that came in through the vents singed and scoured their skin and made it raw. On such a day, the tribes say that the sun is the liver of the sky, smoking with pain. Away to the north, the sky was darker, almost purple.

'You see?' said Leila, 'You see that? Someone is getting wet at last.'

Poor Mercy occupied me, off and on, over a period of some ten years. By the time its publication was being negotiated, Darfur had almost begun to seem like history – until it sprang into ghastly prominence once again in 2004. I was working on the final editing of the novel when *The Scotsman* began running front page headlines denouncing genocide in Darfur. Topicality is a mixed blessing; there have been moments when I have considered sending the Government of Sudan a card thanking them for their publicity efforts on my behalf, but more often I felt wary; it can be frustrating watching a work that was so long in the making being viewed in the press purely in terms of relevance to current news. 'Writing to the moment' carries the risk that, when that moment in world events passes, the writing may be forgotten.

An aspect of the novel which will not, I believe, date in a hurry is the matter of the aid agencies. These are quite extraordinary bodies. The NGOs, the 'non-governmental organisations', are precisely that: non-governmental, undemocratic, unelected, unanswerable to anyone but their own boards of trustees, and yet largely unquestioned. They are a bizarre feature of our society and, I think, far too little studied. They make, for example, a wonderfully convenient proxy for government – as the novel's principle British character, field director Xavier, soon realises:

> Xavier, on his grass-rope bed under the massy black night sky, found his head too heavy to lift, so full was it of worry. As this supposed crisis had developed, Xavier Hopkins had seen that he was a fall guy of peerless quality, Grand Master of the Most Illustrious Order of Patsies; it was, if nothing else, a steady position. For if the Government in Khartoum really had let its people slide into starvation, why then, an aid agency was the very thing to blame.

Does the aid actually do any good? This is a bitterly contentious topic, but in many instances the conclusion has to be that it does harm. Think of Ethiopia, which in the mid-80s was torn apart by war with secessionist Eritrea, and then by famine famously described as 'Biblical' by Michael Buerk reporting for the BBC. The response was wonderfully generous, but many people who have looked at the effects of the resulting Live Aid campaign have concluded that the Ethiopian government used the aid food with colossal cynicism as a honey-pot to lure populations to the camps, and then to shift them in trucks out of the war zones to the Government's advantage, with great suffering on the way and possibly 100,000 deaths. The aid agencies must have had some idea that this was happening, but they said nothing – except for Médecins Sans Frontières who were thrown out of the country for their pains.

Even where the right food is supplied, the actual amounts are often virtually worthless. In Darfur, during famine after famine in the eighties and nineties (including the one I witnessed), each family actually received no more than a few kilos of food aid grain, amounts that can have made no serious difference to anyone. A study commissioned by Save The Children concluded that the people had simply tightened their belts, searched for grubs and berries, roots and herbs, and had survived as best they could, independent of any 'relief'.

But relief will be sent, whether or not it is welcome or whether it makes any difference. The US government, for example, is obliged to disburse a certain quantity of food aid every year, by law. They just have to find somewhere to send it. The machinery is in place, the staff are waiting.

In my old university town there is a pub called The Volunteer. Hanging outside is the traditional painted pub sign showing the traditional redcoat soldier with his musket. Walk past the pub and look back, however, and you see that the reverse of the sign is different; it shows a white medical student vaccinating an African villager. The received meaning of 'volunteer' has changed; in our society, it is now the aid worker who is the institution, and in some cases unhealthily so. Some years ago, a play called *A Map of the Heart* (by William Nicholson) ran in London's West End. One of the characters is the medical director of a relief operation, a woman known internationally as 'the Angel of the Camps,' a figure we readily recognise from such real-life figures as Claire Bertschinger who became famous for her heroic work during the Ethiopian crisis, and who wrote in her memoir *Moving Mountains* that she had long had a taste from adventure and crisis: 'I wanted to be the first on the spot whenever there was a disaster in the world, as a disaster relief coordinator.' Aid workers can be extraordinarily brave and selfless people, but they can also be addicts – disaster junkies – who perpetuate the situation they came to solve. In my own play *Topokana Martyrs Day* back in 1982 I had described this:

> *Ibis*: I recall the parties when we wound up in Biafra, everyone looking lost, wondering what the hell they'd do

211

with themselves now. Someone started singing, 'We'll meet again.' Then someone else said that Bangladesh was looking bad and we all cheered up.

There are several such figures in *Poor Mercy*, people who get high on their own heroic charity.

In *Topokana Martyrs Day* I had come up with a phrase: The ghastly inescapable lightness of the offer of help. The notion that people might not want our charity is unpalatable. But we cannot help meddling, and if you believe that such meddling is new, or that the common view of Africa as a basket case is new, think again. Charles Dickens knew this: Mrs Jellyby (*Bleak House*, 1852) is jolly well going to sort out the starving natives, whatever they may think, and the Jellyby family can go hang while she does so. I have on my shelves a leather-bound volume called *West Indies,* poems published in London in 1809 to celebrate the abolition of the slave-trade (the so-called abolition, one should say; the trade is alive and well today). The poems are unreadable bombast, tedious pentameters depicting noble Albion freeing Africa from its chains, and the book is 'embellished with engravings from pictures painted by R.Smirke,' which name feels appropriate. Greater interest lies in the book's title-page dedication:

To the Directors and Governors of the Society for Bettering the Condition of the Natives of Africa.

But in 1809, almost no one in Britain had ever been to the interior of Africa; just three years earlier, Mungo Park had died in the attempt. Therefore, almost no one had the foggiest idea of the condition of the natives – but already there was a Society for Bettering it. We have not ceased meddling since, and the week before *Poor Mercy* was published (March 2005), the report of Tony

Blair's Commission on Africa appeared, once again telling the Dark Continent what is good for it.

In the novel, the preoccupation of field director Xavier Hopkins is whether there is actually a famine, such as might remotely justify the invasion of Darfur by aid agencies. He is belaboured by messages and demands from the Western capitals and the donor agencies: Is there a famine? There must be a famine! Find it! But Xavier cannot find it; the evidence is not there. He looks back at a previous intervention in the country – the disastrous military campaign of 1883 led by General William Hicks in the pay of the Egyptians – and is forced to ask himself the crunch question:

> On Xavier's desk the reports clamoured, also the accounts, the interim this and provisional that, but the ink was furry where it had sunk into cheap foolscap and his eyes were drifting out of focus. This plethora of words helped nothing. The terms were too narrow, the questions too petty, compared with that devastatingly simple challenge put in his mind by Colonel Hassan al-Bedawi: Should we be here at all?

Poor Mercy is not (I hope) a humourless tract but grimly funny, a humane account of a human situation. I've tried to offer more than a passing response to a moment's crisis. After all, the meddling will continue long after I am forgotten.

MICHAEL RIVIERE - Mutability in Norfolk

> To end here, in this region,
> Long seemed appropriate
> To one who has made of it
>   Almost religion.
>   (*Dilham*)

The region in question is Norfolk, and the author of this verse was a Norwich man who turned himself into a country squire. Michael Riviere, the son of a doctor, worked for a brewery in Norwich and then in London and Belgium, but in the mid-70s retired early to the life of a gentleman, at his large brick-built Victorian house in the north of the county and there dwelt among his books and pictures, spending much of his quite modest funds on 18th century Italian engravings. As a young man there had been sailing, shooting and point-to-points also – he rode well – but in later life he was not strong. Very thin, very tall (his legs longer than the horse's), he had a weak heart and in middle age became increasingly frail. Thus, with time, he grew ever more quiet and still.

The house, Dilham Grange, stands in a few acres of wooded ground on a gentle slope above a small lake. It is a pleasant if not an especially beautiful Victorian red brick house, but it is singularly peaceful, which was very much to Riviere's taste. It enabled him to pay close attention to his inner ear, and the ceaseless refining of his poetry. This small body of poems has proved remarkably enduring. They offer a curious, poignantly anachronistic picture: a poet of the sixteenth century islanded in the late twentieth.

How did this come about? Michael Riviere's life had certainly not been all rural placidity. He began reading English at Oxford, but in

1939 he volunteered and was swept up by war. He served in the Army and was caught in the debacle of Crete in 1941. He escaped from two camps, so was consigned to Colditz along with three hundred of the more bloody-minded PoWs. Of the poems he wrote there, one in particular has often been anthologised. It describes the German sentries' inability to hold the prisoners entirely:

> Unheard, invisible, in ones and pairs,
> In groups, in companies – alarms are dumb,
> A sentry loiters, a blind searchlight stares –
> Unchallenged as their memories of home
> The vanishing prisoners escape to sleep.
>
> (*Oflag Night Piece*)

The military tradition was strong in the family: in a downstairs toilet at Dilham hung a small framed chart illustrating the skill with which Riviere's submariner father-in-law outmanoeuvred and sank a U-boat. But there was also a long commitment to the arts. His grandfather, Briton Riviere, was a Victorian academic painter, a specialist in animals. In Briton's grandiose canvases, lions pad about in classical ruins and white chargers bear Christian knights into gloomy forests; the interest is entirely on the horse. Michael Riviere's own tastes were considerably more sophisticated. The engravings he bought were by Giambattista Tiepolo, he was a Fellow of the Society of Antiquaries, and his library contained splendid folios of neo-classical architectural prints, while his culture-heroes were the great patrons of the Italian Renaissance, Leo X and Duke Federigo of Urbino, that ideal of the civilized prince:

> The mature man, proven and vigorous to mount
> A horse a woman or a muse with the appropriate skill;
> Like Theseus not concerned merely to live, and to have lived,
> But to leave a hero's mark, a palace, an invention, an example,

215

To carry the defiance of Time a little beyond Death.

> (*Urbino*)

Riviere's own defiance of Time became increasingly fastidious, disdainful of fashions, enthusiasms, fads, politics. He could seem like a latterday Montaigne, immersed in contemplation, discarding more and more that failed to meet his exacting standards, not least his own poems. He revised and tinkered endlessly and, if something could not be perfected, it was dropped. The corpus of verse that he would acknowledge shrank steadily as he saw failings and excesses in his youthful work; the *Selected Poems* contains just twenty-two pieces, and these are all that he thought worthy of preservation. Here is one of the very few pieces from his Romantic vein that survived the cull:

All Summer through
The gods of loin and eye
Riotously pursue
The glimpses of her hair and shoulder
In forests from whose startled foliage
Like doves the spiritualities fly.

But when the green
Is scythed away with snow
Only her eyes are seen,
And one God stands declared, to link us
In this transparency of Winter
With neighbourly angels to and fro.

> (*Seasonal Love*)

I think that Robert Graves and W.H.Auden may also have visited that particular wood.

Dilham Grange and its life are described in close detail in his son William Rivière's novel *Echoes of War,* in which the men of the family are conflated into one, a portrait painter. The image that Riviere himself cultivated was elaborate: he preserved a coat of arms and an Italian motto: 'Sprezzatura'. The word translates most readily as 'nonchalance', but with distinct undertones of 'disdain, contempt'. He cultivated an interest in one of his ancestors, a Huguenot (which he insisted on pronouncing with a final 'knot'). When he lit the log fire in the drawing room, he would leave the door open just for a minute, so as to give the air a delicate taint of wood smoke. There were moments when one caught a hint of self-parody, of a tongue slyly buried in the cheek – except that Riviere was so tall, one could never see it clearly enough to be sure.

But there was also seriousness about scholarship, the arts, a measure of civic duty (he chaired committees for the University of East Anglia), a thorough knowledge of his locality, all focused on the country house. And not just his own, but across Norfolk:

> ...some rare
> Country houses where
> More than the land
>
> Is farmed, quiet halls and manors
> That have, in metaphor,
> Stood two millennia
> As lamp-bearers:
>
> Places Xenophon
> Or Horace would have recognised,
> Or Ronsard, as civilized...
>   *(Dilham)*

The contemplation of country houses and the values they enshrined became part of the theme that came to dominate his writing, and which in the 16th century would have been called 'mutability'. It is a theme with which English Renaissance poets – Spencer, Daniel, Lea and others – grappled repeatedly. The great concern is the passage of Time. What does Time erode? What does it preserve? What does it change, or mutate? How might we, our behaviour and our works, come through its slow sifting? Does the shoring up of a gentleman's values offer any defence? How should we face up to death? In poem after poem, Riviere returns to Time and mutability as to an obsession, and frequently the setting is a country house. In *Rippon*, the Hall is serene and the effect Yeatsian:

> We had stopped to eat blackberries when we heard horses
> And the three Miss Birkbecks arrived, riding back to
> the house,
> Talkative, sunlit, beautiful, all on grey horses.
> Those moments, had a painter been there, might have
> lasted generations

A painter, note; for Riviere, a photographer would not have done. But the artist was elsewhere, and the image is lost to Time. In another 'house' poem, he considers his old friend Robert Ketton-Cremer, scholar and last of the Felbrigg squires:

> Families have no beginning, but can end,
> Though 350 armigerous years
> Brighten the vellum...
> Here in his great library, ill and slow,
> He leans between his lamp and the young moon
> (*Felbrigg*)

The slowness, the illness was something Riviere recognised only too well. When I visited Felbrigg Hall some twenty-five years ago, certain rooms were preserved in aspic, the books and papers on the desk, 'just as they would have been the day Mr Ketton-Cremer died', as the guide assured me. Perhaps they still are, though this handful of dust tossed in the face of Time seemed faintly ludicrous. But while recognising that the very oldest English families are nonetheless the prey of Time, Riviere revered the 350 'armigerous' (i.e. entitled to a coat-of-arms) years of the Felbrigg squire's family. Contemplating the end of those celebrated Norfolk Renaissance correspondents the Pastons, he grieves that –

> Eternity of blood's no longer, as once,
> Any man's confident possession.
>
> *(On Lady Katherine Paston's Tomb)*

It is a consideration one can hardly imagine occurring to a more contemporary poet.

Though Time will certainly get us and our heritors too, retreat to the country at least slows the decay, the erosion. But with age one has to face up to the poor sum of what one is. In a sequence of short verses called *Late in the Day*, written when he was only in his early sixties, he considered his oncoming frailty:

> It needs 'honesty and courage
> To face the change' (of age)
> Writes Eliot, and seldom a poet
> That's man enough to do it.

Absorption in one's own decay in old age is, again, hardly a fashionable theme and might seem to us rather self-obsessed. But it was a theme that the 16th century mutability poets returned to repeatedly:

Far from triumphing court and wonted glory
He dwelt in shady unfrequented places,
Time's prisoner now…
A man-at-arms must now go on his knees.

The words, in fact, of Sir Henry Lea, courtier-poet to Queen Elizabeth I, writing *circa* 1603 about his own extreme old age; they might have been written by Michael Riviere *circa* 1980.

In the countryside, at least, one might escape the trammels of a bewildering, dishonest modernity, and be –

Clear of all that mars content,
Commerce, radio, government

(*La Boëtie: Ce jourd'hui, du soleil*)

This comes from a translation, one of a number that Michael Riviere made from the French poets of the 16th century, particularly the Pléiade circle or, in this case, from Montaigne's great friend Étienne de la Boëtie. The insertion of radio tells us that these are 'versions' rather than with strict renditions. One notes the very specific disdain; radio's particular crime was to be noisy: for Riviere, silence was decidedly golden. The one art he had little feeling for was music, which was seldom heard at Dilham. He preferred the ticking of a clock, or that potent consolation for those oppressed by mortality, the sound of children playing in the garden.

Riviere had a great love of the French Renaissance poets, Ronsard above all and, in Ronsard, particularly those poems that dwell on a withdrawing from the world:

My park-gate's locked, and town house door.
I'm not subscribing any more.

(*Ronsard: A Rémy Belleau*)

220

Not that Riviere would have wanted a town house. Ronsard's Mignonne poems (of the 'gather ye rosebuds while ye may' genre) perfectly suited Riviere's notions of fragile beauty at the mercy of Time. Here is his version of one of these:

> Let me love you in the sun
> Now, while weather holds, Mignonne.
> Roses fast as chances die,
> And vice versa, so it's said.
> Age will dapple that dark head
> Soon, almost, as spring's gone by.
>
> Time's in flower. Field and wood
> Prompt this harvest of the blood.
> Death, like lovers, has his wish:
> Just as – look – we strip again,
> Tongue to tongue and vein to vein,
> He will strip us of our flesh.

> (*Ronsard: Cependant que ce beau mois dure*)

Here are mutability and death once more, expressed with a melancholic sweetness. For Ronsard, and for Riviere, translation was itself a defiance of Time:

> Anacreon made poems of
> Inseparable wine and love:
> I drink to him, and those true men
> Who by their translations have
> Fetched him back out of the grave,
> English Cowley, French Estienne.

> (*Ronsard: Nous ne tenons en nostre main*)

Riviere's admiration of Ronsard has its ironies, since the Frenchman was a Catholic zealot who would have had little time for the Huguenot Rivieres, and who included musical scores with some of his published poems, being notably keen that they should be set to music as indeed they often were – something that would have set Michael Riviere's teeth on edge. One notable difference, indeed, between the French originals and Riviere's versions is that the latter would probably resist musical setting. With its dense, clipped syntax, its predilection for heavy enjambment of the line ending (not an especially marked feature of the Pléiade), and its sometimes rather packed punctuation, Riviere's verse reads better than it sounds and can be a little thick in the mouth, perhaps the consequence of repeated re-working. But to my mind, the translations from Ronsard are very good indeed, Riviere's finest work. They achieve a nonchalance, a sprezzatura. The playful business of translation, of teasingly updating the Renaissance poet, liberates him from solemnity. In his excellent rendition of Ronsard's *De l'Election de son Sepulcre,* he has the shepherds sing of Ronsard, that he was:

> A man who, when alive,
> Never had to contrive
> Contacts or introductions
> To important persons;
>
> Used no obsequious tricks
> On fashionable critics:
> Employed no druggery, buggery
> or skulduggery.

Ronsard, a glittering young aristocrat, had no need of cultivating anyone. Had the younger Riviere, in his 1950s Poetry London days, employed a few more such tricks, he could have been more 'famous'. He would have scorned any such thing, but might sometimes have wondered, ruefully.

222

For a man so inclined to melancholy contemplation, what part could art play?

> Artists do no more
> Than interrupt time a little,
> Though they use blood itself to colour
> Verse, palette or score
> (*On the Limitations of Art*)

But, at the same time, through the voice of Ronsard (deftly 'Englished'), Riviere evokes the great poets and marshals them in the face of Time:

> We Life-creating Dead
> Perfect those skills with which
> We made earth rich:
>
> Sappho, fished from the sea
> Into eternity;
> Marlowe called from backgammon,
> Herbert from Heaven…
>
> The Muse alone may cure
> Sad hearts of this world's care,
> And flatter the failing spirit
> With dreams to inherit.
> (*Ronsard: De l'Election de son Sepulcre*)

In one of his own poems, Michael Riviere achieved a charming, light-hearted fortitude in the face of death. It is a piece from his twenties, written in his first PoW camp, but it has little of the war about it. Rather, it seems remarkably prescient of his later career:

> Well, Riviere's dead. Muffle a smallish drum,
> Beat it in a small way, let us be apt and just.

223

Small stir kept step with him and can see him home
Very well. The firing party? Simplest
To brief some children for a pop-gun squad.
Art (though he wrote some poems) seems none the worse.
He was in one battle, but unfortunately on the side
That lost. Once managed to ride round a steeplechase course
(Unplaced). Riviere is dead. Look moderate solemn,
Walk moderate slow behind his seven-foot corpse
Who was a half-cock, pull-punch, moderate fellow,
And symbol of so much and vain expense
For years carried pints and gallons of blood about
To manure this casual, stone-sprouting plot.
        (*Eichstätt*)

Michael Riviere died in 1997, more than fifty years after writing this. As Ronsard wrote elsewhere, 'It's time to leave houses and orchards and gardens, vessels and plate which the craftsman engraves, and to sing one's passing as does the swan.'

(*Note:* I later discovered that someone has, in fact, set Michael Riviere's verse to music. This was the Italian composer Franco Donatori. The group of settings is called *Late in the Day,* for soprano, flute, clarinet and piano. It was first performed in Norfolk in 1992 by the Logos Ensemble with soprano Sara Stowe.)

CORVACEOUS

1. WINNIE & BELLOW

Two days a week, I go to Dundee University as a Fellow of the Royal Literary Fund. It's such a grand title that I've been agitating to have it replaced with 'Pooh Fellow', since it is all paid for by Winnie the Pooh.

The Royal Literary Fund has been in existence since the late 18th century, helping out impecunious authors; Coleridge was an early beneficiary. More recently, the Fund inherited and then sold to Disney the rights to A.A.Milne's work. This produced a colossal sum of money which must be spent in charitable or educational ways. At about the same time, there was rising disquiet about the state of writing in British universities; students didn't seem to know how to do it. So, now, the RLF pays for professional writers to assist by seeing students individually. We will help anyone, British or foreign, from undergraduate to lecturer in any faculty, who has problems with academic writing.

And they have plenty. Some are floundering badly out of their depth, and it can be difficult to keep a straight face at times: a design student wrote that, 'In every age, jewellers have included materials appropriate to the age, for example stone in the Stone Age and metal in the Metal Age.' Some imagine that they must sound like distinguished professors, and so load their text with indigestible dross. An economics student who came to me kept referring in essays to 'individuals operating in the commercial environment.'

This, I discovered, meant 'people shopping'. The student looked dismayed. 'But I have to sound like an economist!' she wailed.

There are considerable pleasures in the work, not least the great variety of humanity one meets: I have a particular liking for oil and mineral law Masters students from Kazakhstan, always bright and friendly. Exchange students – Norwegians, Dutch, Germans – on the European Erasmus programme can be very clever and sharp witted. Some people, however, simply shouldn't be there. Last year in particular, the University was awash with Chinese Masters candidates, many of whom could barely speak or write intelligible English. Why do they come? Because British universities need to milk the £10,000 annual fee, and the students get a certificate to take home, apparently regardless of what they comprehend. Thankfully, that influx has ended.

We RLF Fellows (there are about 150 around the UK) have a restricted access website on which we can discuss the problems we face and how to deal with them. Recently, a colleague described an MSc candidate whose dissertation was impossibly bad, and remarked how dispiriting it was not being able to help them. Other Fellows replied with stories of students offering inducements for 'help' – i.e. someone to write their thesis for them.

I've been here before. A long time ago, in the 1970s, I was sent by Voluntary Service Overseas (VSO) to a city in Java, working in educational publishing. A Chinese girl called Winnie came to see me. She was studying English at one of the local universities, and she couldn't manage the dissertation. For some reason, she had chosen to write on the novels of Saul Bellow. The subtleties of Chicago Jewish irony were completely lost on Winnie; she hadn't a clue what he was on about. Rather reluctantly, I agreed to help her – at least, to discuss the novels with her. But as time began to run out, she was

226

obviously still struggling; she couldn't make head nor tail of *Dangling Man, Seize the Day* or *Henderson the Rain King*.

Winnie became desperate. The degree was terribly important to her. Her family were anxiously waiting for her to graduate, and then to find the job that would lift them all out of poverty. She could see that she was going to fail, and all she could think of was to get me to write it for her.

The presents began: it started with tins of lychees, and eventually I realised that she was offering me more intimate favours. When she came to my house, she would sit with her typewriter on the table, looking up at me expectantly; whenever I attempted to 'discuss' Saul Bellow's fiction, she would simply type everything that I said. It soon became terribly clear that I was, in effect, dictating her dissertation.

At last it was done, and Winnie submitted the typescript. A week later, she was told that she'd failed, because she'd clearly had too much help. I felt foolish and responsible, and was worried about her: would the shame perhaps drive her to self-harm? Would her family shun her – or worse?

I needn't have worried: Winnie was more resilient than I'd guessed. Very quickly, she acquired a new boyfriend. His name was Peter, and he was an Australian military attaché. Before I knew it, Winnie was married and living in Melbourne. This is not a solution open to most clients of the Royal Literary Fund in Dundee.

2. TROUT

Down in Sussex, old friends are making arrangements for a summer party. The family are direct Bloomsbury descendants, and the annual gathering celebrates all that was, and still is, silliest about Bloomsbury. The year I was there, the focus was on Virginia Woolf, and the silliness was beyond belief.

Few writers are easier to mock than Woolf; from her contemporary Wyndham Lewis onwards, there have been plenty of eager parodists. The received impression is of a woman infinitely gloomy, precious and self-obsessed, agonising over dinner menus, art and the cosmos all in one breath. It's an image that grieves her living relatives. Her nephew Quentin Bell recalled her as a gregarious, fun-loving woman whose family adored her because she made them laugh.

Fun and parody persist each summer at *The Quentin Follies*, named in memory of Quentin who died in 1995 and who was himself an endlessly kind and witty man. This festival of the cheerfully ludicrous and more lighthearted arts is held each July at Charlston, Bloomsbury's Sussex retreat, created by Quentin's parents Clive and Vanessa Bell. There, in the pretty gardens, pictures are auctioned to raise money for returning Charlston to something like its former self. The works on sale are of a uniform size, and are donated by a galaxy of contemporary talent. From beside the pond, a balloon race is launched; the prize my year was a genuine Quentin Bell table lamp with, swirling about the base, three concupiscent naiads in lustred pink and grey ceramic.

At dusk, the crowd gathered with hampers and bubbly in a large marquee fitted with a miniature proscenium arch swiped from English National Opera. Here we enjoyed cabaret of a most unusual sort.

The evening was seamlessly compered by Quentin's son-in-law, author William Nicholson. It began with great charm: a clutch of children, who'd been at work with circus teachers all afternoon, showed how they could now juggle and walk the high wire. I played a bit part with two of the littlest Bells helping me to sing 'The Tattooed Lady'. A star turn was Dennis Healey who recited a parody of Stanley Holloway entitled 'Michael and the Leon', its jibes at Messrs Hesseltine and Britten a tad dated but deft and witty nonetheless. None of these, however, could quite prepare us for the Neo-Naturist Cabaret.

We had become aware, as we milled about in the proceeding hour, that a small group of women (in, I think, their forties) were sitting behind the marquee stark naked, and were painting themselves and each other with colourful swirls and paisley-patterns of blue and green. Stepping in due course out onto the stage, these ladies announced that they were to give the assembled family and friends of Bloomsbury a representation of 'The Suicide of Virginia Woolf'.

Which they did. The painted lovelies held up crude placards announcing the acts of the drama, such as: 'Virginia goes to the river and drowns herself.' At this point, two of them (both playing Mrs Woolf) entered wearing nothing but calf-length woolen cardigans. They filled the ample pockets with pebbles taken from a bucket, and lay down on stage to drown. All the while, one of their colleagues sang 'Poor Tom is Dead', tunelessly, over and over.

Then a new placard was held aloft which read, 'Virginia's Soul is Reborn as an Iridescent Trout.' At this moment, the two drowned Woolfs shed their cardies and stood upright in all their naked paisley splendour. We now saw that each wore a large plastic sweety jar, held securely in place over the mons pubis by generous lengths of sellotape. From these, they proceeded to take fistfuls of boilings, which they lobbed out into the audience.

All the while, the voice continued to intone, 'Poor Tom is Dead'.

What, you might wonder, was the audience thinking? By now there was a thoughtful hush, except for a few dogs and children playing outside the marquee. Quentin's daughter Cressida, who had been moving among the tables selling Toblerone, stood rooted to the spot. Glancing to my right, I saw her sister Virginia and their mother Olivier watching in dignified, expressionless silence. Remarkably little was said by anyone.

At last the evening continued with songs, conjurers and tableaux. As a finale, the Neo-Naturists returned to the stage and attempted to lead the audience in Community Singing of 'On Ilkley Moor bar t'at'. Curiously, the only people who joined in were me and Dennis Healey. We gave it laldy, but either no one else knew the song or they were still too gobsmacked to raise more than a whimper.

Should you wish to attend the next Quentin Follies, a quick Google will find you the appropriate website, with images of the artworks for auction. It's great fun. I'm told that, since the Neo-Naturist Cabaret, acts have been clamouring for a slot.

3. WUTHERING

Back in the spring, I taught an Arvon course. I've done a few now, usually at the Arvon Foundation's centre at Moniack Mhor near Inverness. Arvon creative writing sessions take a standard format: sixteen customers come for a residential week and are helped (or not) by two tutors who are professional writers. The students do the cooking, while the tutors hold workshops and individual sessions. It can be great fun.

Sometimes I have taught 'Writing from Life', and the students tend to be persons of a certain age who have issues that they wish to write out; frequently, this turns out to be a rocky relationship with their parents, maybe decades ago. This can be stressful for the tutors; sometimes the student doesn't really know what they want to say, which makes it difficult to write well. A lot of grief can come to the surface. But there can be surprises too; one young man – eastern European, and very gay – stomped about in a temper half his week, smoking and muttering that he didn't know what he was doing here, since he wrote in Russian anyway. But suddenly he began scribbling, and on the last evening read out an extraordinary account of a gay orgy in Belarus, a country where homosexuality does not officially exist.

The recent course was quite different. This was in Yorkshire, at Lumb Bank, a house once owned by Ted Hughes. The students were 14-year-olds and came from a school in Glasgow, on an estate with a dismal reputation. I was told that they were 'bright but culturally deprived'.

Before the course, I felt decidedly apprehensive: how well would I relate to these young people? My co-tutor was a delightful Irish poet. Leanne O'Sullivan is twenty-five, sassy and ebullient and pretty in an wonderfully Irish way, with a mane of wavy golden hair, a wrinkling freckled nose and green eyes. She comes from a big farming family in County Cork, and she writes about sex and bulimia. Before reaching Yorkshire, I was convinced that I was doomed: the Glasgow kids would immediately empathise with Leanne. The girls would identify with her, while the boys wouldn't be able to get to sleep at night for thinking about her. What time would they have for an old fool like Falla? Some of my anxiety must have reached Leanne, as she sent me cheerful emails telling me to stop worrying.

In the event, the Glasgow kids could not have been nicer. Some came from thoroughly dysfunctional families but, as far as we were concerned, they were polite, they were fun, they were interested. They did all the cooking. Leanne taught them poetry, I taught stories. The notion of doing nothing but write for a week they found weird, but by the Friday they had produced an anthology of stories and poems and held a 'launch' at which they all performed. There were nights when they didn't sleep, but that's because they were giggling.

The whole ambience must have been strange to them. The Arvon house at Lumb Bank is full of handwritten poems by famous names, framed and on the wall, together with dozens of signed photographs; I slept in a room with a Fife friend, Kathleen Jamie, smiling down at me. In the dining room, there's a huge and rugged photo of Ted Hughes. In the village just up the lane, Sylvia Plath is buried in the churchyard. I don't think the kids had heard of either Hughes or Plath, but the atmosphere began to touch them.

As it did me. The house sits on a steep hillside, with a deep valley dressed in oak and beech trees below. It must have been a mill-owner's home, and there is industrial archaeology on all sides: ruined mill pools, chimney stacks and canals. It takes little imagination to visualise gangs of malnourished mill workers in wooden clogs heading for their fourteen-hour shift, trudging up and down the steep paths on paved lanes (passing a decent distance away from the owner's door).

Not far away, over the moor, is the Brontë parsonage at Howarth. Again, I don't think the kids had heard of any Brontë but, on my morning off, I decided to walk there. It is about fifteen kilometres over the hills, so I set out at 6.30 a.m. with a flask and sandwiches, thinking to get a bus or taxi back at lunchtime.

But I got wuthered off the heights. By mid-morning, I was climbing up a steep muddy track into cloud with horizontal rain coming at my face, and I gave up. Not, however, before I had passed a house that looked the perfect model for Cathy and Heathcliff's home. It was a substantial farm once: solid, two-storey, with massive lintels and mullions and many outhouses. But the roof had collapsed, and the rain had darkened the stone to near black. The empty windows stared out at the rain scouring the moors. It was difficult to imagine any warmth or love in such a house.

When I got back, the kids were unimpressed by my account. Leanne led them up to the graveyard and read them a Plath poem at the graveside. What notion they'd gained of the literary life, I don't know, but we felt quite emotional sending them back to Glasgow.

4. FIRST DRAFT

I will soon complete a raw first draft of a new novel; the next stage is to think about sending it out to one or two trusted readers. This is an awkward moment for any writer. One wants an email in return that same evening declaring, 'This is a work of genius!'

Something of the sort happened to Dostoevsky. He delivered the manuscript of *Crime & Punishment* to his publisher and (the story goes) that same night was woken by pebbles tossed at his window, and the publisher in the street crying, 'It's a work of genius!' (prior to ripping him off in the contract). Last time round, my loyal father did ring two days later, and pronounced my piece a work of genius, but then admitted he'd only read 59 pages.

One cannot necessarily control the point when a first draft must be declared 'done'. It may simply be a matter of exhaustion, or a feeling that a fragile structure has been edged together which, if we don't inspect it now, might fall apart. For everyone's sake I want my readers to look at something that is as good as possible, but there always comes a moment when I cannot touch another word without having some other's reaction.

The choice of readers is delicate. They must be willing: why should anyone want to read 300 pages when we all know from the outset that it could be better? They must be competent, for the novel's future may depend on what they say. They must be sympathetic but not too kindly, for one needs help, not flattery. Ideally they know something of publishing, to tell you if the work is saleable or a waste of time. But one must be very careful not to try their patience, for one may need them again, and how often can you ask someone to re-read a long novel?

Trust and a little professional distance are required. As a young poet I enthusiastically swapped verses with a close friend and we responded in every over-the-top way, sometimes heaping extravagant praise, sometimes ripping to shreds. We were in the process of working out our own artistic values. Some while later, I asked this friend to read the typescript of my book on rebels in Burma. The comments that came back were precise and invaluable but too rude, sometimes mocking; I lashed out in ungrateful anger and, for a brief while our friendship suffered.

And then what? Write it again. My first novel *Blue Poppies* went through five drafts. Even now, after several editions, I all too readily spot sentences that are ugly, clumsy or just plain wrong, and I curse, asking myself what on earth I was doing on each revision?

The answer, usually, is that I was cutting. Writers know that one must be prepared (in Arthur Quiller-Couch's phrase) to 'murder your darlings'. The favourite sentence, the prize paragraph that makes one purr with pride on re-reading: that is the one that is almost certainly redundant, or over-wrought, or calls too much attention to its own style. A favourite author of mine is the Anglo-Argentine naturalist W.H.Hudson who wrote about 19th century Patagonia. John Galsworthy thought that Hudson wrote 'as though an angel is whispering in his ear', and remarked, 'Goodness knows how this fellow gets his effects.' That's what I want.

In Norman MacLean's novella *A River Runs Through It* (filmed by Robert Redford) a father teaches his sons to write. When they submit work for his approval, he remarks (at least, in the film) encouragingly, 'That's very good. Now do it again half as long'. When they come back next day, he approves the shortened version – then says again: 'Much better, but bring it back tomorrow half as long.' There is no more important lesson for a writer. In revision drafts I do my best to strip away words that are showy individualists, and leave instead a tight, interdependent whole. I'm usually only too happy when a friendly editor points out the blunders. My boarding school, which was founded in the 1890s with strong links to the Arts & Crafts movement, had a sonorous motto of which William Morris would certainly have approved: *Work of each for weal of all.* Not a bad rule for books, either.

So, with a first draft of the new book done but three or four revisions still to come, you'll understand my nervousness as I consider who to ask to read it.

HISTORICAL FICTION AND THE MORAL AGENDA

For many years, historical fiction was looked down upon as consisting of little but reheated war stories, heavy-velvet Tudor tales, or cozy portraits of golden-hearted folk in the back alleys of Salford and Glasgow. Nostalgia, a love of dressing up, and a yearning for a world of more simplistic social relations – it's all part of the taste.

But there has always been more to historical fiction than this, many other motivations, agendas, and risks. And we can surely agree on one thing: a large percentage of what is called literary fiction is in fact 'historical'. *Beowulf* is set in what, even for its first audience, would have been an historical period, far enough in the past to have mythic qualities, close enough to be identifiable. It is remarkable how true this is also of the great canon of 19th century novels. *War & Peace* describes events that took place some sixty years before the time of its publication, well before Tolstoy's birth. *Wuthering Heights,* that iconic early Victorian novel published in 1847, in fact describes events that only culminate in 1801 before Napoleon became emperor, events which begin thirty years earlier still, around 1770 – it is curious to think of *Wuthering Heights* as an *ancien régime* tale. Many of George Eliot's novels, quite apart from *Romola* set in Renaissance Italy, look back several decades: *Middlemarch* is set around 1830, forty years before it was published. Thomas Hardy's *Mayor of Casterbridge* is set – again – roughly forty years before his date of publication, while his *Return of the Native,* published in 1878, carries a preface informing us that:

The date at which the following events are assumed to have occurred may be set down as between 1840 and 1850, when the old watering place herein called 'Budmouth' still retained sufficient afterglow from its Georgian gaiety and prestige to lend it an absorbing attractiveness to the romantic and imaginative soul of a lonely dweller inland.

Maybe the Victorian market felt the same nostalgia for old clothes as we do today. But also, when looking back one or two generations, it is possible to believe that we have a more distilled and objective view of how society operated then – easier than trying to make sense of and write about our own times. The social issues back then seem clearer: the coming of industry, rural backwardness, urban poverty, electoral reform and change generally. Society cries out to be understood, and just as an anthropologist may look at primitive communities because the waters are less muddied, so for some authors of historical fiction, the past may seem clearer than the present, and may offer a key to understanding where we are now.

Certain historic settings carry an almost Pavlovian emotional and moral response: just mention that the troops are whistling as they march merrily towards a river in France, and readers feel an awed thrill, murmur 'the Somme', and give a nod to 'the futility of war'. But great events offer the author a chance to grapple with the most serious and moral issues imaginable. Here, for instance, is Tolstoy in *War & Peace*:

> On the twelfth of June, 1812, an event took place opposed to human reason and to human nature [The French invasion of Russia]. What produced this extraordinary occurrence? What were its causes? ... The more we try to explain such events in history reasonably, the more unreasonable and incomprehensible do they become to us.

And so on. Tolstoy is seeking to understand not just historical events, but History itself, and Destiny.

Similarly, when it comes to the great sequence of chapters describing the pivotal Battle of Borodino, Tolstoy tells a cracking story, but is chiefly concerned to show how far events were beyond human control – even Napoleon's control. Whole chapters are given over to analysing this.

Tolstoy rarely apportions either blame or credit to individuals, but he strives to understand why events turned out as they did. Considering the Battles of Borodino and Austerlitz in particular, he concludes that any attempt to point the finger at Napoleon, or Czar Alexander, or whoever – any such attempt is fatuous, because (says Tolstoy) no one is in control of the rolling tide of history and fate. The Russian and Austrian allies lost at Austerlitz, he claims, because men fought for pointless goals such as glory and fame; the Russians won at Borodino because of moral superiority. Here is what he writes in *War & Peace*:

> It was not Napoleon alone who had experienced that nightmare feeling of the mighty arm being stricken powerless, but all the generals and soldiers of his army... The moral force of the attacking French army was exhausted. The victory of the Russians at Borodino was not that sort of victory which is defined by the capture of pieces of material fastened to sticks, called flags, or of the ground on which the troops had stood and were standing; it was a moral victory that convinces the enemy of the moral superiority of his opponent and of his own impotence. The French invaders, like an infuriated animal that has in its onslaught received a mortal wound, felt that they were perishing.

Tolstoy does not believe in grand strategy, or great leaders, or national destiny. He goes the other way. He writes:

> Only by taking infinitesimally small units for observation... the individual tendencies of men... can we hope to arrive at the laws of history.

This is the realm of the novelist: seeking for the universal in the particular, in the sufferings and personal triumphs of individuals.

That relation between the individual and the great tide of history is a recurrent theme in historical fiction. But it did not please the next generation of Russia's rulers, the Soviet regime; they wanted portrayals of class struggle. Boris Pasternak's *Doctor Zhivago* was first published in 1957, in Italy, from a manuscript smuggled out of Russia by the journalist Sergio d'Angelo. 1957 was forty years – that magic forty years again – after the Revolution of October 1917, which cataclysm occurs in the novel largely off-stage. Pasternak's long cast list includes people from every class, from wealthy bankers in fashionable society to peasants and railway workers, none of them especially better or worse than any other, and all of them helpless in the face of uncontrollable events, just as in *War & Peace*. In *Zhivago* even seemingly powerful people – such as Komarovsky the lawyer-turned-politician who seduces young Lara, or Pasha the student idealist who becomes a ruthless military chief doomed for being too successful – these figures too are finally helpless and are destroyed by something out of control. This was not good Marxism. *Zhivago* was refused publication in the Soviet Union and, according to Sergio d'Angelo, on passing over his typescript Pasternak said, 'Consider this an invitation to my firing squad.'

As Rick Blaine says at the end of *Casablanca:* 'The troubles of three little people don't amount to a hill of beans in this crazy world.'

Tolstoy and Pasternak might have added that when the little people are engulfed by a veritable landslip of beans one has a moral duty to dig out the corpses and give them a memorial.

Across the Atlantic, the American Civil War has produced many novels, and here the issues are different. It has been remarked that the Americans love their civil war like no other, for its high moral tone of liberty and emancipation, and its position in the story of the nation.

The Battle of the Crater is a novel by Newt Gingrich, the Republican speaker of the House of Representatives who bid for his party's nomination to fight Barack Obama for the presidency. Gingrich's novel takes particular slants on history, none of them well supported by fact. The real Battle of the Crater was fought in June 1864, at the end of the Civil War. For Gingrich a central figure is the Union General Ambrose Burnside, whose troops dug a deep mine under Confederate lines with the notion of blowing these sky high before charging in. The plan went horribly wrong; the mine blew a splendid hole but did not pierce the Confederate defences; it simply made a huge crater. Union troops poured into this crater where they were trapped and shot with ease by the Confederates; they were packed in so tight that accounts speak of 'the standing dead'. In Gingrich's novel, General Burnside is a visionary whose plan is undermined by the meddling of the galumphing big bureaucracy of the Union army administration. And if there is one thing Newt Gingrich the Republican politician hates, it is bloated bureaucracy and a meddling administration, the speciality of Democrats.

Meanwhile, Gingrich in his novel defuses the worst criticism of the Confederate troops made at the time: that they slaughtered black prisoners indiscriminately. Gingrich draws a veil over that, but has instead the sainted Confederate General Robert E. Lee issuing an

241

order that black prisoners are to be treated equally to white. In reality, Lee never issued any such instruction – but Gingrich is a Southerner, and when he published in 2011 it was election time, and what better way to endear yourself to voters of the American South than to polish up the image of Lee and the basic decency of rebel troops?

At the same time, Gingrich – as a Republican – could associate his name through his novel with the Civil War and all its defining mythology. The war was, after all, a time in which the Republican star burned brightly progressive; they, not the Democrats, were the party battling for the emancipation of the black slaves. Here we have a politician writing historical fiction to associate himself with a particular high moral tone.

Of course, not every episode in history has a high moral tone, and where matters of shame and guilt are involved, the question of individual participants becomes more complicated, because if there's one thing on which every critic and creative writing course today seemingly agrees, it's that good fiction must present characters with whom we can identify.

Several well-known novels about India cover the Amritsar massacre of 1919, often cited as one of the worst stains on British colonial history, in which possibly a thousand civilians including women and children were shot by Indian troops under the command of General Reginald Dyer. You may recall that Prime Minister David Cameron visited Amritsar and paid respect to the dead, calling the episode 'deeply shameful'. He declined, however, to apologise officially on behalf of Great Britain saying that, 94 years on, apology was inappropriate. Whether or not one agreed with the Prime Minister, one might also feel that something the fiction writer could do was to offer an account of events if not as apology, then as some sort of restitution. The event is brought back into the public consciousness, made vivid, made memorable – and is thus not forgotten.

What about fictional versions? In Salman Rushdie's *Midnight's Children,* the Amritsar massacre is witnessed by an Indian doctor who is saved from being shot by fortuitously sneezing, so that he falls down and is missed by the bullets. The episode is brief in the novel, and when the doctor gets home his wife asks: 'Where have you been?' to which he answers, 'Nowhere on this earth.' Rushdie by no means ignores or disguises the episode. But, in a curious way, he does disarm it. He makes it farcical, he makes it unreal, and he sidesteps the question of complicity. We are not witnessing – in Hannah Arendt's famous phrase – the banality of evil but, if you like, the risibility of evil.

In Paul Scott's *Raj Quartet* novels, the Amritsar massacre is recalled by the widow of a British army officer who cannot free herself from her memories, or from her experience of having been reviled when she refused to contribute to the legal fund in defence of General Dyer, giving instead to a relief fund for the Indian families. Here, a let-out is being offered to the reader, who may sidestep their own discomfort at the historical atrocity by identifying with a solitary, faintly mad but sympathetic old lady, an oddity, an outsider. If we identify with her, then we are not identified with the racist society that produced the massacre.

Scott's *Raj Quartet* books now seem to us to be historical fiction, although it should be remembered that they were written and originally published in the 1960s and early seventies, only some twenty years after the culmination of events leading to Indian independence. The theme running through Scott's novels is the racism that was all-pervasive during the British Raj, and its corrosive effects on both British society and Indian. The issue of personality is complex here; the young Indian hero, Hari Kumar, is the embodiment of everything bright, progressive and open minded, and it has been suggested that Hari represents everything that in Scott's own life was crushed by his upbringing. By contrast, the villain of the piece, the policeman Merrick, is the embodiment of torment: bisexual, sadistic, racist, he reflects many of Scott's own personal problems – his uncertain sexuality, his hard-drinking and his tendency to violence, his dis-ease with racial difference – and his attempts to confront these.

But again, notice the effect of hanging these attitudes on a particular fictional character. Just as we recognise the wickedness of Merrick's sadistic racism, we are also repelled by him as a character – physically repelled when he returns from fighting the Japanese with his face badly disfigured. We are invited to understand and to criticise all those attitudes and policies which made the British Raj unacceptable, but at the same time we are given a character to hang them on from whom it is made as easy as possible to distance ourselves.

In one well-known passage, Merrick's own true Britishness is questioned in a surprising way. Interrogating a terrorism suspect, Merrick speaks the man's language – literally so. Merrick turns out to be a first class linguist. Other British observers in the scene, hearing him use the native tongue in such an idiomatic fashion, feel that he goes too far; they feel a fastidious revulsion as they listen to what they regard as Merrick's excessive fluency. Once more, Merrick distances himself from us, the reader. We British don't really speak foreign languages, we are not quite like that – and thus Paul Scott again slyly lets us off the hook.

Frequently in historical fiction one finds a similar process letting us escape too immediate a feeling of guilt: historical novels often carry within them a portrayal of some gross historical injustice, while the style of the writing is in important respects comical or absurd. Matthew Kneale's *English Passengers,* which won the Whitbread Prize in 2000 and was shortlisted for the Booker, concerns a farcical expedition by religious enthusiasts in 1857, sailing from London to locate the Biblical Paradise in Tasmania; the novel also relates the destruction of the Tasmanian aboriginal population. The book is undoubtedly vivid, but the tone seems to me problematic, turning the motivations, justifications and character of the British colonists and enthusiastic clergy into something to mock. The narrator of the Aboriginal story is a mission-educated half-caste. His account is measured, reasonable and poignant. The actual English passengers are an ill-assorted bunch of religious zealots and incompetent smugglers, the stuff of comedy. It is clear with whom one is intended to sympathise. But sympathy is not identity. The Aborigine's account is given in an invented patois, littered with jokey and inept linguistic coinings. He is not like us. Thus an historical crime is explored – but again we the readers are protected from too much identification with either side.

After all, if you hope to sell a large number of copies of your novel to a certain audience, it's maybe not a good idea to tell that audience to despise themselves and their forebears.

There are other ways of addressing an historic injustice, while both engaging the audience but simultaneously insulating them. In 2000, Peter Carey's *True History of the Kelly Gang* won a string of prizes, including the Booker and the Commonwealth Writers Prize. Ned Kelly in his suit of home-made armour and his Sidney Nolan paintings already constituted a folk hero for Australia. Carey's idea was to take Kelly back to his childhood, to his roots among poor Irish settlers much abused by the British authorities, showing how Kelly's gang and their struggle with the police was the result of oppression as much as of criminality. Various motifs in the book suggest that a level of truth beyond the merely factual is being explored: in his first-person narration, Kelly frequently rhapsodises over the night sky and the great clear arc of timeless light above, even as the petty thieving and disputes close in around him. The language of his telling has a mildly prudish dignity. Kelly's account of his own escapades is presented through the device of a series of fictional documents, confessions if you like, supposedly scribbled on various bits of scrappy paper shortly before his death. Ostensibly, this documentary presentation gives the story a reality and a *raison d'être*. But it also distances it: the documents are presented as archival, as museum curios. The literary machinery insulates us from them.

So, we see a few common factors. Every novelist knows to present sympathetic characters. Each of these books offers the reader such a character: the old lady and the doctor recalling Amritsar, the aboriginal recalling Tasmanian genocide; the young Irish bandit in Australia. But in each case the degree of identification is controlled and limited. Few of us are likely to feel full identification with any of these people who in their different ways offer a deep criticism of our own history. Nor will many of us much identify with the villains, with General Dyer, with the ludicrous Tasman missionaries, or the coarse settler society of Australia. A curious moral detachment is achieved, in which injustice is portrayed but also neutralised.

The identification of the crimes of the past with a particular personality in a story became an issue again with the 1995 novel *The*

Reader, by Bernhard Schlink. This is the tale of Michael, a teenage boy in a German city in the mid-1950s – four decades beforehand, you note – his intense involvement with an older woman called Hanna, and his subsequent horror when she is charged with having been a concentration camp guard who, in 1945, was responsible for a group of 300 Jewish women, and who locked them into a church which then burned down in an air raid, killing them all. As the trial progresses, young Michael realises that he holds what may in fact be a key to Hanna's defence: she is illiterate. She cannot read the confession she signs, and during the war and the Holocaust she can only have been dimly aware of what was going on.

This book stirred a mini-holocaust of its own. It was popular worldwide but nowhere more so than in Germany, selling half a million copies, a fact which in itself aroused confusion and suspicion. Many accusations were thrown at it: in particular that, by making Hanna illiterate and tormented, Schlink was attempting to draw the reader into sympathising with her. Meanwhile, the illiteracy appeared to be a metaphor for the moral illiteracy of the German people as a whole who – it was implied – were thus in some degree ignorant of the horrors that they were caught up in and were perpetrating. This – so hostile critics such as Frederick Raphael argued – was arrant nonsense: one would have had to be stunningly stupid not to have known what was going on in Germany in the 1930s and 40s. For a start, Hitler's frequent radio broadcasts made literacy almost irrelevant. So it was argued. It is interesting that *The Reader* appeared at much the same time as Daniel Goldhagen's celebrated and controversial historical study *Hitler's Willing Executioners,* a widely-read and provocative book arguing that ordinary Germans knew very well what was happening, and promoted it. What strikes me here is how Schlink's achievement, in humanising the evil into one woman with a problem, was seen as morally reprehensible on the one hand (by Jewish critics such as Raphael in particular) and hugely popular on the other hand, among German readers.

For this is what novelists do: we create a character who embodies a conflict or dilemma, and we make them as human as possible. Is it possible that, in the process, we may excuse evil too much? *Comprendre, c'est pardonner* – but maybe fiction has no business excusing crimes as appalling as the Holocaust. We have a paradoxical situation here: novelists bring history to life by peopling it with believable characters who enact our darkest sides. But in the process, we may disarm the case for the prosecution, whether by making those caricatures farcical (in *English Passengers*), or morally and physically revolting (in the *Raj Quartet*), or humanly afflicted, as in *The Reader*.

This danger can be seen in factual history writing also. A study by Mary Fulbrook called *A Small Town near Auschwitz* (2012) deals with the true-life career of a young man called Udo Klausa, head of the local bureaucracy of the region around the concentration camp. Klausa was not involved in murder or torture; he was a functionary who pushed papers because that was his job. He claimed that he knew nothing of genocide and witnessed little. But there is a counter-accusation: that German civilians at the time went through a process of what has been called 'performing their conformity and acquiescence' – which is to say, they put on an act, colluded in a self-serving way, telling themselves that they were preserving their inner beliefs and humanity, while balancing these against what they were required to do, and all in a manner which they hoped let them morally off the hook. The *Times Literary Supplement* review suggested that the historian's attempt to understand Klausa's motives really gives the official more leeway and more credit than he deserves; said the reviewer: 'The line between explanation and exculpation is a very delicate one.'

It could be argued that merely by drawing attention to a moral outrage in the past, one is to some extent righting a wrong, making good, atoning. In Ian McEwan's novel *Atonement,* this process becomes the fiction: in 1935 a thirteen-year-old girl witnesses and misunderstands a glimpsed encounter between two would-be lovers, and the results are disastrous. The young man, Robbie, is wrongly accused of a rape, is jailed, and is only let out in order to join the army, as a result of which he is fatally wounded and dies at Dunkirk. The young lady is permanently alienated from her family, and is killed during the Blitz in London. Only later does the child witness realise who the rapist really was, but this man has married his victim, and his wife cannot testify against him. So our witness – who *mirabile dictu* becomes a famous novelist – later in life makes amends or seeks 'atonement' by writing a last novel in which the young lovers are given the happiness they were denied in life.

So that's all right then. Quite what the dead victims might have thought of this deal, this atonement, is not explored. Possibly only a crime created in fiction can be absolved by more fiction, and only a novelist would consider that the writing of a novel constitutes justice. Nonetheless, this is what some historical fiction is doing: atoning for past injustice. Is the righting of distant wrongs not a matter of setting up a straw man and whipping him hard? What good does it do today's aboriginals in Australia to have Matthew Kneale 'atone' for their destruction in Tasmania in the 1870s?

If, however, you bring your history more up to date, there is another risk: today's 'guilty' society may resent it. This is particularly a peril if you are a foreigner. I am an Englishman in Scotland. My own novel *Glenfarron* contained passing mention of Clydeside shipyard workers who, during WW2, attacked Polish refugees looking for work. Mentioning this brought down the wrath of one reviewer who declared that I was out to get the Scots for being racist. In my next novel, *The Physician of Sanlúcar*, the villain happens to be another Scot and is responsible for the slaughter of natives on Tierra del Fuego *c.*1900. The character is based on a documented historical figure known to infamy as Mr McInch. It is not my mission to force Scotland to confront historical guilt, nor do I especially want another spat with that reviewer. But am I not to tell this story? Or should I cravenly change the nationality of Mr McInch, the culprit? You see the problem: making your audience uncomfortable doesn't go down so well. One notes the absence from modern British fiction of many novels about more recent shameful episodes in British history, for example the Mau Mau rising in Kenya and its vicious suppression. There is a famous novel about Mau Mau entitled *Weep Not, Child* – but it's not by a British author. It's by a Kenyan, N'gugi wa Thiongo. Across in West Africa, there are some fine novels about the destructive effects of British colonialism on African society, but they are by the Nigerian Nobel winner Chinua Achebe, not by any British writer. So there is plenty for which we might yet make amends.

Other novelists face the hostility problem in far greater measure than me. Another Nobel winner, the Turkish author Orhan Pamuk, received death threats and was prosecuted a few years ago for speaking up about the massacres of Armenians in Turkey between 1915 and 1923, a crime that Turkey still finds it very difficult to acknowledge. Pamuk has written historical novels, but this is a subject that he has not touched in fiction. It is difficult to blame him; it seems unlikely that such a book would find a Turkish publisher. It is all very well for our Louis de Bernières to write of the Armenian genocide – in *Birds Without Wings* – but for Pamuk the Turk it might be impossible.

There is another variety of hostility worth mentioning: the view that some historical events are too serious to be regarded as mere fodder for story-telling. This was particularly the case with the Holocaust, and there is a view that fictional portrayals of the death camps are grotesque, invalid and fraudulent. I don't suppose this is a view that many here [at the historical fiction festival] would share, but you may feel that using another country's suffering for your own fictional purposes is, at least, morally interesting.

In August 1944, with the war in Italy going against them, four companies of German SS troops arrived in the Tuscan village of St'Anna di Stazzema, and proceeded to murder everyone they found: 560 people were killed, brutally. They included many women and children, the youngest a baby of just 20 days. It was one of the worst atrocities of the war in Italy, and those basic facts are not disputed.

What is disputed is why it happened. After the war, just one German officer was prosecuted, and even he was released after only a few years. With no more court statements by witnesses, something of a veil of silence fell, with neither the Italian nor the German authorities doing anything to lift it. Diplomatic and trade relations, and the reconstruction of Italian democracy, were too important to have the boat rocked either by high profile trials of Germans, or by exposés of the role of Italian Fascists. But by 1994 the political climate had changed – and it now happened that a steel cupboard was found in the basement of the military authorities in Rome, which had been turned face to the wall. It was christened 'the cupboard of shame' because it was found to contain some 600 files concerning the massacre. So the story again came into the open, and

251

the Italians put various elderly Germans on trial *in absentia,* unable to get them extradited from Germany. So far, not so bad.

But in 2002 the black American novelist James McBride published his story *Miracle at St'Anna,* in which the massacre is discovered by, would you believe, a small group of black American troops. These soldiers also discover that the Germans were led to the village by a traitor in the Italian resistance. The black Americans now heroically fight to defend the village from a German counter-attack, and all but one are killed. This appropriation of an Italian tragedy to spotlight Afro-American heroism was, for some sensibilities, quite bad enough, but then McBride wrote a script from his novel which was filmed by the black American director Spike Lee.

Even before the film was released, there were loud protests in Italy that both film and novel traduced the memory of Italian resistance fighters who, it was insisted, had certainly not led the Germans there. The received Italian version is that the massacre was unprovoked, terror for the sake of terror, nothing to do with the Resistance. However, it's not that simple: it is known that early on the morning of the massacre, someone in the village spotted a German signal flare, at which all the able-bodied men in the village scarpered into the woods, leaving their families undefended. It was women, children, the elderly and the animals that died, not the young men.

The row over St'Anna di Stazzema grumbled on. But my point is this: the novelist and the film maker had a moral agenda that was about redressing an injustice, but not the injustice of the massacre: their concern was the injustice of how the role of black Americans in WW2 has been ignored – and in that cause, they produced a film with little basis in fact.

One might say: never mind. They *did* highlight the neglected story of the black soldiers. They *did* in the process bring St'Anna to international attention again. And, perhaps more importantly, they *did* also highlight the complicity of some Italians – an uncomfortable matter which many have difficulty accepting, a wound that might never heal unless the truth is faced.

James McBride made no apology for his version. He declared: I'm a writer of historical novels, not history books.

It's worth comparing all this with the experience of William Styron, the white novelist from the Southern state of Virginia, whose 1967 novel *The Confessions of Nat Turner* concerns a slave insurrection in Virginia in 1861, an historical event. Styron was met with a barrage of criticism from black American writers who objected to his appropriation of 'their' story. 'Is it possible [wrote one] for a white Southern gentleman to tune in on the impulses, beliefs and thought patterns of a black slave?' Another wrote an essay entitled 'You've Taken My Nat and Gone.' So the historical novelist was now cast as a thief. [The events of 1861 were in 2016 re-cast as the film *Birth of a Nation* by another black American actor/director Nate Parker – some sort of restitution, perhaps, not least in confronting the title and concept of the grossly racist 1915 film of the same name by D. W. Griffith, one history redeeming another a century later.]

Back to Russia, and to a different sort of historical fiction. Vasily Grossman's epic *Life & Fate* (dramatised in 2015 on BBC Radio 4) is an account of the Great Patriotic War against Nazi Germany, and was aimed at correcting the distortions of Stalinist propaganda.

You may fairly object that *Life & Fate* is not an historical novel at all; Grossman started writing it in 1959 – that is, only fourteen years

253

after the end of the war, basing the story on events he had lived through himself as a correspondent, particularly the siege of Stalingrad. But there is another sense in which Grossman did perhaps perceive that he was writing an historical tale. The novel includes vignettes of both Stalin and Hitler, but also every variety of Soviet citizen, 160 characters, depicting their experience of and their part in historical events. In his project to set the record of the war straight, to correct the official lies, Grossman seems to be establishing what we might call a baseline for history, a bedrock for our understanding, a fundamental story for all writing that follows.

Other novelists have done the same thing. The 1959 book *Exodus* by Leon Uris became the second-biggest fiction seller in the USA after *Gone With The Wind*. Again, you might disallow this as historical fiction; Uris was a Jewish-American journalist who had covered the Arab-Israeli fighting of 1956, while his story is set in 1947, just a few years beforehand. Nonetheless, as with *Life & Fate,* there is in *Exodus* what feels like a self-conscious attempt to create history, to get the proper story established from the outset – the foundation story of the state of Israel.

There is a disputed account of the genesis of *Exodus*; it is said that a certain Edward Gottlieb, a Jewish public relations man in the US, commissioned Leon Uris to write the novel to do just that: to create an epic story of the founding of Israel that would cement in American minds the notion of an heroic, virtuous struggle with which any right-thinking person could identify. True or not, the book is regarded as having had a huge influence on US attitudes to the middle east. In the novel, the only good Arab is a dead Arab – literally so: the good Arab dies – and in some quarters this attitude towards Arabs endures today.

Thus, historical fiction may be fiction that establishes a history: 'This is who we are. This is how we have staked our claim on history.' And Leon Uris and Vasily Grossman would surely have agreed with Tolstoy on one thing: our side won because we are morally in the right.

Producing a morally correct foundation story didn't help Grossman: *Life & Fate* went down no better with the Soviet authorities than Pasternak's *Zhivago*. Publication was blocked, and Grossman was told by an official, 'This book cannot be published for another two hundred years.' The authorities not only confiscated every copy they could find, they even destroyed the ribbons from Grossman's typewriter. Grossman – who died in 1968 – never saw his book in print. Having been smuggled out to the west, it first appeared in English in 1980 and in Russian in 1988, some four decades after the events.

Spain is another country where the publishing of historical fiction has had its problems. For several decades after the Civil War, any attempt to publish books critical of Franco's regime would have got you nowhere except perhaps prison. There were certain oblique commentaries in films such as *The Hunt* (1966) and *The Spirit of the Beehive* (1975) but a corrective historical work like *Life & Fate* was out of the question.

Of course, times have changed, but bad historical memories still have unpleasant force; like Turkey, Spain still struggles with the legacy of its past. When Franco died in 1975, the transition to democracy was facilitated by something known as the 'Pact of Forgetting'. This was essentially a legal amnesty on bad memories, intended to make it possible for old enemies and their children and grandchildren to go on living together. But this abolition of memory proved immensely difficult. For a start, the families of those

255

murdered by either side wanted to know what had happened to their kin, and to find where they were buried. In the year 2000, a grouping was formed with the catchy name of the Association for the Recovery of Historical Memory. About the same time, a group of Spanish novelists began producing works of 'historical memory', focussing not just on the events of the Civil War, but on how the memory and the history has been handled since. The best known of these is the novel *Soldiers of Salamis* by Javier Cercas, which describes an incident when a Francoist prisoner should have been executed by a Republican soldier, but was not; the novel then seeks out the soldier who did not shoot, to understand the anomaly.

The continuing importance of clarifying memory is illustrated by what happened next. In October 2007, sixty-eight years late, a Spanish Socialist government passed the famous Law of Historical Memory which dealt with the aftermath and victims of the war, providing for a variety of correctives, atonements and makings-of-amends, so that (for example) exiles could at last regain their Spanish nationality. Sensitivities, however, were still very raw; Conservatives in Spain had opposed the law from the outset. One of the legal provisions paid for the exploration and opening of suspected Civil War mass graves. In 2013, Spain's Conservative Prime Minister, Mariano Rajoy, halted state funding of the grave explorations, citing economic hard times. This was the climate in which novelists such as Javier Cercas and his colleagues felt it essential to keep writing, because other people may co-opt your history for their own ends.

Here for example is the publicity blurb for an historical novel called *Wayfarers of Fate* (2006):

> Against the grim backdrop of the Spanish Civil War, we watch as Juan and Pedro Avila choose their different paths. Brother is set against brother as the maelstrom of war carries

them away. Juan strives for the Communists, and falls in love with the beautiful Hilda Krantz, a deadly Communist agent. When she betrays him he fights on, though wracked with cynicism and despair. When he finally stands over his brother's body on the battlefield, he comes to see the barrenness of the Communist cause and redirects himself towards the light.

It may not surprise you to learn that the author, John Steinbacher, was a well-known conservative Catholic commentator in the USA.

In a lecture given in 1988, the Peruvian novelist Mario Vargas Llosa argued that it is the business of novelists not to tell the truth, but to lie as powerfully as possible, so as to create a self-sufficient world and the best possible story, and to present their understanding of humanity – and history, and truth– as forcefully as can be.

In fiction, historical truth and moral truth are not the same thing at all. All historical novels are lies; they are, for instance, full of made-up conversations which cannot be true. We can live with that, but there is another artistic problem which can for some readers be a moral problem: many historical events are, in terms of good fiction, poorly structured. In most of our own lives, the key moments happen in the wrong order, the important players in our story come and go at un-dramatic moments, the rising tension is haywire and the climax happens in our teens. To make a good story, things must be re-ordered. For certain audience groups, this is not acceptable – especially if they have a stake in the story. The Hollywood script consultant Linda Seger recounts how she was commissioned to work on a film telling the tale of the founding of the Mormon state of Utah in 1846; it's that urge to cement the founding history again. The problem for Linda Seger was that the Mormons would not tolerate any deviation from historical fact. In one instance, a dramatic sequence had to be rewritten. In another, to strengthen the drama, Seger had placed a speech by the church's leader Brigham Young on the wrong side of a river, prior to an epic crossing. Many of us here, I suspect, would find such adjustment of the truth excusable in fiction if it made for a better story. But to the Mormon church, it was unacceptable.

Here's a last contrast: of all 20th century British novelists, few were more closely associated with a conservative religious outlook than the staunch Catholic, Evelyn Waugh; he, for example, strongly resisted the re-writing of tradition at the 2nd Vatican Council of the 1960s. Surely such an author would be a stickler for historical truth, at least as regards his religion. Evelyn Waugh wrote just one historical novel, *Helena,* published in 1950, which deals with the early Christian church in Byzantium. He gives the novel a preface in which he confesses that he altered certain facts for the sake of the story. He concludes with this:

> The novelist deals with the experiences which excite his imagination. In this case, the experience was my desultory reading in History and Archaeology. The resulting book, of course, is neither History or Archaeology... The story is just something to read.

SPECTRUM

Each summer I run a month-long school of creative writing for St Andrews University, most of the students being young Americans. When they prepare assignments, I ask them to consider the typeface they will be using; I insist on a serif face, but encourage them to try something other than Times New Roman, the default on most computers. TNR was designed, I suggest, to enable plenty of words to be packed clearly into narrow newspaper columns; it was never meant for books, and appears ugly and cramped on the book page. It is no accident that few good books are printed in TNR. Please, I say, look for a typeface more beautiful, more pleasurable to read. Look at Garamond, look at Caslon, please look not just at the words you write but the letters that carry those words. For my part, I cannot conceive of wanting to write well without thinking how the text will appear on the page. I would as soon serve malt whisky in a styrofoam cup.

I've thought this way since I was old enough to pull books from my parents' shelves. My family owns two volumes of Milton's poems printed by Emery Walker at the Doves Press in London around 1905, in the unique typeface designed for the press – exquisite books, in which every letter has been placed upon the page with honour, although the type had a startling end when the owner of the press, T.J.Cobden-Sanderson, in a temper threw the letters into the Thames; some were recovered by divers only in 2016. Walker and Cobden-Sanderson's style of typography was exceptionally clear and uncluttered; Milton's words shine off the heavy paper with no more decoration than large red capitals for the headings. My father, seeing my interest, gave me another book, an unusual Gospels printed in Dordrecht in 1665; it has parallel text, one column in Anglo-Saxon, the other in Gothic, the latter using possibly the first Gothic font ever cut. I have it on my desk today.

I began to wonder if I should be a printer. In the 1970s, as a student at Cambridge, I was shown round the Rampant Lion Press of Will and Sebastian Carter. In their cramped but impeccably tidy rooms, with the massive hand-pulled presses gleaming black and a smell of spirit lye everywhere, large sheets of printed work were hung overhead to dry.

'Look,' they said, 'here is print that has been done on dry paper. It is clear and crisp, but look carefully and you'll see that the letters sit upon the face of the paper. Now look at this sheet: the paper has been gently damped before printing and, as it dries, the ink is drawn slightly into the body of the paper, to become part of it. That is fine work.'

I left Cambridge and in 1978 went to work in the city of Bandung, in Java, for a local publishing company. They were printers also, and in the basement printing hall an offset litho machine was the only modern presence. Under Dutch rule, this had been the First Bandung Steam Printing Company, and there was a row of small platten presses formerly powered by an overhead shaft driven by steam. More spectacular were two massive Heidelberg flatbeds dating from the 1920s. On these, the company printed school textbooks on large sheets of cheap paper, sixteen pages at a time. The broad iron bed packed with heavy metal type lay out in front of the machine. It would slither on a greased track back under a roller the size of a tree trunk which carried the paper, before the mechanism slammed into reverse and the type-bed reappeared at the front. The press must have weighed a ton or more, and the sheer momentum of the type-bed heaving in and out was visibly inefficient, a colossal waste of energy but glorious to watch. The Heidelberg was fixed to the concrete floor with hefty bolts but it looked as though it must tear itself from its mounts at every pass. The Javanese staff called it the *Dukun* – the Witch.

The company's cheaper publications were bound with hot glue, but others were hand-stitched in a back room by half a dozen demure ladies in long batik skirts, gossiping in low voices. Typesetters worked at the keyboards of rattling pre-WW2 Linotype machines producing strips of hot metal text for the Witch, but for small jobs there were wooden cases of old Dutch cold metal type; it is possible that some of these fonts were rare, manufactured in the famous type-foundries of the Netherlands but long since extinct in the homeland. Elderly Javanese gentlemen with spectacles and black caps shuffled in leather slippers through the printing hall or worked at high benches setting type in hand-held trays. Remembering the Rampant Lion in Cambridge, I asked if they would teach me. Can you be serious, their faces asked – a young, so-modern westerner wanting to learn our obsolete skills?

Indeed I was serious. For much of my two years there, I would go in of a Sunday morning and spend an hour or two setting type – poetry, usually – before attempting to print my work on the small platten presses. I was very bad at it, and the courteous old gentlemen would indicate patiently that my letters were upside down, or that I was creating blots by over-inking. Or I would print fifty sheets painstakingly, spread them out to dry, and then smear the lot by sweeping them up too soon, not appreciating how slowly ink dried in the tropical humidity of Java. But what a lovely and calming occupation it was; so much so that, four decades on, the memory is as clear as a line of Garamond print. In 1980 I wrote from Java to the Rampant Lion in Cambridge asking if they ever took on apprentices; they told me to go to college.

Just then, as a young author, I was looking for subjects for fiction. The history of 20th century Indonesia is a tale of violence, not calm, and the owner of the print and publishing firm had played shadowy roles during the War of Independence and thereafter; one evening at his house I found myself dining with another courteous old gentleman in a batik shirt, but this time an army general who had been a key figure in the Revolution, and in the coup and the bloodbaths of 1965.

It was, however, a different real-life figure who finally caught my imagination; he was a Dutch soldier who, during the independence struggle, switched sides and fought for the nationalists. My fictionalised Dutchman stays on in Java and learns to print, just as I had done, in a basement works full of crashing Heidelberg presses. With four novels commercially published previously, I had good hopes for this, but perhaps a story of revolutionaries and printing in Java was over-taxing the British readership. Finding a publisher proved awkward, and I almost gave up.

Then, four years ago, with my family I went on a barge-and-bicycle holiday through the Netherlands and Belgium. In Antwerp one day I took myself off to visit the Plantin Museum – the home and workshops of Christophe Plantin, 16th century master-printer, in whose honour the 1913 Plantin typeface is named. Beside an austere courtyard and sombre chambers whose walls are lined with tooled leather, there are Plantin's print-shops with wooden flatbed presses of the variety he and his labourers once used. These were tiny, slow machines compared to the iron Witch in Java; for Plantin's men the working day was long and hard. And as I peered at these presses, a solution to my problem presented itself.

Will Hill is a typographer and teacher in Cambridge; I've known him since boarding school fifty years ago. He had once foolishly said that he would design a book for me, by way of exercising his craft. So I took him up on it. In February 2015 we saw the result, a novel called *The White Porcupine*, and yes, it concerns printing and terrorists in Java and Holland. It is hardback, with a lovely cover design based on batik fabric, and the text is set in Spectrum, a face designed by the Dutch typographer Jan van Krimpen around 1945. We have had one hundred and fifty copies printed for private distribution, signed and numbered by the author and/or the designer.

Meanwhile I've no idea what became of the firm in Java. Even while I was there it was in trouble; the owner died, and his property was fought over by his two wives to the point of paralysing the company. Salaries (already meagre) went unpaid, and staff drifted away. I expect that, in the years since, the Witch has been dismantled and sold, and the cases of antique Dutch type probably discarded, perhaps even thrown in the Cikapundung river. In the pages of the novel at least, the ancient gentlemen work on in silence.

25080003R00155

Printed in Poland
by Amazon Fulfillment
Poland Sp. z o.o., Wrocław